C000006930

1 MONTH OF
FREE
READING

at
www.ForgottenBooks.com

By purchasing this book you are eligible for one month membership to ForgottenBooks.com, giving you unlimited access to our entire collection of over 1,000,000 titles via our web site and mobile apps.

To claim your free month visit: www.forgottenbooks.com/free206750

* Offer is valid for 45 days from date of purchase. Terms and conditions apply.

ISBN 978-0-331-81264-0
PIBN 10206750

This book is a reproduction of an important historical work. Forgotten Books uses
state-of-the-art technology to digitally reconstruct the work, preserving the original format
whilst repairing imperfections present in the aged copy. In rare cases, an imperfection in
the original, such as a blemish or missing page, may be replicated in our edition. We do,
however, repair the vast majority of imperfections successfully; any imperfections that
remain are intentionally left to preserve the state of such historical works.

Forgotten Books is a registered trademark of FB &c Ltd.
Copyright © 2018 FB &c Ltd.
FB &c Ltd, Dalton House, 60 Windsor Avenue, London, SW19 2RR.
Company number 08720141. Registered in England and Wales.

For support please visit www.forgottenbooks.com

Harvard Depository
Brittle Book

COLET   ERASMUS AND MORE

OXFORD REFORMERS

SHAW   1895

941.45
Shaw

Harvard Divinity School

ANDOVER-HARVARD THEOLOGICAL
LIBRARY

MDCCCCX

CAMBRIDGE, MASSACHUSETTS

INTRODUCTORY LECTURES

ON THE

OXFORD REFORMERS

𝕮𝖔𝖑𝖊𝖙, 𝕰𝖗𝖆𝖘𝖒𝖚𝖘 𝖆𝖓𝖉 𝕸𝖔𝖗𝖊.

Delivered in Philadelphia, in 1893, under the auspices of the
American Society for the Extension of
University Teaching.

BY

W. HUDSON SHAW, M.A.,
Fellow of Balliol College, Oxford

PHILADELPHIA :
THE AMERICAN SOCIETY FOR THE EXTENSION OF UNIVERSITY TEACHING.
1893.

PRICE, FIFTY CENTS.

INTRODUCTORY LECTURES

ON THE

OXFORD REFORMERS

Colet, Erasmus and More.

Delivered in Philadelphia, in 1893, under the auspices of the
American Society for the Extension of
University Teaching.

BY

W. HUDSON SHAW, M. A.,
Fellow of Balliol College, Oxford.

PHILADELPHIA:
THE AMERICAN SOCIETY FOR THE EXTENSION OF UNIVERSITY TEACHING,
1893.

COPYRIGHT, 1893, BY
THE AMERICAN SOCIETY FOR THE EXTENSION OF UNIVERSITY TEACHING.

941.45
Shaw

ANDOVER · HARVARD
THEOLOGICAL LIBRARY
CAMBRIDGE. MASS

Ha57- 02016

LECTURE I.

———

John Colet.

" A good man was ther of religioun,
And was a poor Persoun of a toun ;
But riche he was of holy thought and werk.
He was also a lerned man, a clerk
That Cristes gospel gladly wolde preche ;
His parischens devoutly wolde he teche.

This noble ensample unto his scheep he gaf,
That ferst he wroughte, and after that he taughte :
Out of the gospel he the wordes caughte,
And this figure he addid yit thereto,
That if gold ruste, what schude yren doo ?

A bettre preest I trowe ther nowher non is.
He wayteed after no pompe ne reverence,
Ne maked him a spiced conscience,
But Christes lore, and his Apostles twelve,
He taught, and ferst he folwed it himselve."

—CHAUCER'S *Prologue.*

" The awakening of a rational Christianity, whether in England or in the Teutonic world at large, begins with the Florentine studies of John Colet. From the first it was manifest that the revival of Letters would take a tone in England very different from the tone it had taken in Italy. a tone less literary, less largely human, but more moral, more religious, more practical in its bearings both upon society and politics. The vigour and earnestness of Colet were the best proof of the strength with which the new movement was to affect English religion . . . . . It was his resolve to fling aside the traditional dogmas of his day and to discover a rational and practical religion in the Gospels themselves, which gave its peculiar stamp to the theology of the Renascence. His faith stood simply on a vivid realisation of the person of Christ. In the prominence which such a view gave to the moral life, in his free criticism of the earlier Scriptures, in his tendency to simple forms of doctrine and confessions of faith, Colet struck the key-note of a mode of religious thought as strongly in contrast with that of the later Reformation as with that of Catholicism itself."—J. R. GREEN.

LECTURE I.

A T the outset of these three lectures on the Oxford Reformers of the early sixteenth century, it may be well, perhaps, that I should indicate their scope and intention, and explain why I think your time will not be altogether wasted in examining the life-histories of such men as John Colet, Erasmus and Sir Thomas More. It will be my fault surely, and not due to the nature of the subject itself, if you do not recognize in the records of these three lives one of the most interesting and stimulating portions of English history. It is true enough that from the point of view of those historians who care only for war and politics, for the doings of kings and statesmen and diplomatists, these Oxford scholars played a very unimportant part in the world, and are scarcely worthy of notice. They never slew anybody, or gained advantages over their foes by judicious lying, or stole territory that did not belong to them. Moreover, if Professor Seeley is right when he says that history is concerned only with the development of States and has nothing to do with individuals except in their capacity of members of a State, then certainly Colet and Erasmus and More have no special claim upon the attention of historical students. We had better inquire into more important matters, such as the wars of Henry VIII., in France, or the intricacies of Cardinal Wolsey's foreign policy. But those of us who have been unfortunate enough to receive our training in Oxford, that antiquated and Old-world University, that home of lost causes and exploded ideas, who acknowledge as our master in history, John Richard Green, and sympathize alike with the scorn which he showered upon "drum-and-trumpet" theories of historical writing, and his daring heretical attempt to set the figures of the poet and the philosopher, the merchant and the missionary and the discoverer, in places of equal honour with those occupied by princes and warriors, cannot consent to see history narrowed down to a mere branch of politics. It is very improper, no doubt, but I feel certain that the majority of those here present, who care for the study as it bears upon human lives and not as a means of passing an examination or obtaining a degree, find much more genuine interest in the history of ideas and great movements than in the history of wars and treaties and faction fights. You would rather solve the problems of the Renaissance than know accurately all the intrigues and diplomatic schemings of the eighteenth century. The Hundred Years' War of England against France, and the exploits of tinsel heroes like Edward III. and the Black Prince have become inexpressibly wearisome to you. Like Macaulay's criminal, who preferred the galleys for life to the enforced reading of Guicciardini's History, you would rather endure many woes than be condemned for long to the Wars of the Roses. Wycliffe and More, Lord Bacon, Raleigh and John Milton, the men of ideas, are more attractive to you than innumerable brave and stupid fighting barons of feudal times. If this be so,—if there seem to you greater utility in studying the lives of thinkers and scholars who have powerfully influenced the thought of their race, its religion and its morals, than in busying yourselves perpetually about battles and sieges and the doings of selfish conquerors and ravagers,—then these Reformers of four centuries ago will possess for you a strong and powerful attractiveness.

For, in the first place, all three of them were good men as well as great. One hears it said often enough that history is chiefly a record of crimes and cruel deeds, of tyrannies and rebellions, of falseness and turpitude; and that the more deeply read people are in the life of the past the less belief they have in mankind. Certainly if the moral sense has not been dulled by hard experience of evil, if the conscience is still sensitive and delicate, there is pain enough in human records. A life like Henry VIII.'s, or Pope Alexander VI.'s, or Charles II.'s, a book like Machiavelli's 'Prince,' a self-revelation like the autobiography of Benvenuto

Cellini or Rousseau, is a hideous nightmare to most of us, which we would gladly forget if we could. We turn with a sense of relief to the biographies of men like these of whom I have to speak, who, living in a corrupt and immoral time, in that transitional epoch when the Middle Ages were dying and the New World which we know had scarcely come into being, demand little of that charity which historians find it necessary to accord to great men of the past. Emphatically, whatever may have been their faults, Colet and Erasmus and More were, for their generation, the very salt of the earth. It has been claimed for John Colet, who died before the Reformation had fully come to the birth, that he was the founder of that rational Christianity which 'the Teutonic races have in the main accepted. He was also our English Savonarola, scarcely inferior to the great Dominican in courage and boldness, a preacher of righteousness who did not flinch from denouncing the mad war-schemes of an ambitious king or from exposing the worldliness and corruption of the order to which he belonged,—in his own manner of life pure and blameless amid almost universal degradation. Erasmus was not only the most brilliant man of letters of his age, the recognized leader of the scholars of Europe, the Catholic who helped to make possible the success of Luther by his merciless denunciations of monks and clergy; but he was also a man, who in spite of some lamentable failings, wins our admiration by his large-mindedness, by his single-hearted devotion to learning, his scorn of low ambitions, his hatred of war and tyranny and cruelty, his genuine piety and love of goodness. As for Sir Thomas More, it is difficult to speak of him in words which will not seem to you strained and exaggerated. Against him history has one charge to bring and only one. For the rest, it seems to many of us that his is absolutely the most perfect and lovable character in English annals, King Alfred's not excepted. A man of vast intellect and powers, yet of exquisite simplicity: a despiser of pomp and luxury, yet devoted to culture and refinement: courted by kings and princes, yet happy only in his home with his children: the first thinker of modern times, who yearned with passionate longing to ameliorate the lot of the toilers of the world:

More laid down his life at last cheerfully, and in the spirit of a hero and a martyr, for a cause which he judged to be just and right, and which was in truth the cause of English liberty. He was recognized then, and he is recognized now by all historians who are not blinded by religious passion, as the noblest English-man of the sixteenth century.

Secondly, the study of those three lives will bring you face to face with that great intellectual movement of Italy which has revolutionized human existence,—that Revival of Letters which may rightly be regarded as the most important change in the history of Europe which has occurred since the fall of the Roman Empire. We of Anglo-Saxon descent are naturally anxious to know how the Renaissance affected our own race, what influence it had upon the Reformation, in what ways it differed from the Renaissance in Italy. The answers to these questions can best be found in the lives and works of the Oxford Reformers. Colet, Erasmus, and More, with their friends Archbishop Warham, William Grocyn, William Lilly, and Thomas Linacre, were the first leaders of the English Revival of Learning. Through their instrumentality, Florence, the intellectual centre of Europe, the famous city which has effected for the modern world what Athens did for the ancient, brought her influence to bear upon Oxford, and from Oxford the new light was spread over the rest of England. But in the hands of these scholars of Teutonic blood, the Renaissance was strangely modified, and modified in a way that all Englishmen have reason to be thankful for. Contact with ancient literature made them rebels against mediæval religion and thought, but not against Christianity itself. They were untouched by the Paganism of the Italian scholars. We cannot imagine John Colet listening with pleasure, as Lorenzo de Medici did, to a satire upon immortality, or Erasmus refraining, like Cardinal Bembo, from reading S. Paul's Epistles, lest their bad Greek should corrupt his style. " The Revival of Letters in England," it has been well said, " took a tone far different from that which it had taken in Italy, less literary, less largely human, but more moral, more religious, more practical in its bearings both upon society and politics." Nothing is more striking than the manner in which the healthy English conscience assimilated what was good in the Italian movement and rejected the evil. Great as was the enthusiasm of the Oxford scholars for the New Learning, they valued it chiefly as a means to a noble end. Colet learnt Greek in order that he might cast away the fetters of the schoolmen and find in the original documents of Christianity a simpler and purer faith. Erasmus loved culture with boundless enthusiasm, but he used all his learning and scholarship to bring about reform of the Church and nobler views of life. Sir Thomas More, like Machiavelli, wrote a treatise on government and politics, but his free thought produced not a libel upon humanity and a picture of hopeless degradation, but a generous vision of future progress and an exalted scheme of ethics. In fact, the moral element in our English Revival was the predominant one. Colet inveighs against corruption and selfishness in high places. Erasmus lashes the laziness of monks and the tyranny of kings. More dares to dream of a time when poverty and misery shall' have vanished from the earth, and obedience to the laws of Christ shall have brought about a veritable kingdom of God amongst men.

And thirdly, we have an additional source of interest in the fact that we have to deal with the epoch of the Reformation,—of the " Lutheran tragedy," as Erasmus called it. In that tragedy these men played their parts. The Reformation saddened and gloomed the last days of Erasmus and obscured his fame ; it brought More to the scaffold in the prime of life. In a certain sense they had prepared the way for Luther, and were precursors of the Reformation ; nor were the monks altogether wrong who complained that Erasmus had laid the egg which Luther hatched. But the Oxford Reformers were no Protestants. Their chief importance in history is to be found in this, that they had given to the world an alternative scheme for a reform of the Church by quiet, gradual methods, without a revolution. They failed. Luther succeeded. He destroyed the abuses and corruptions of the Church, but the price paid was the sacrifice of the unity of Christendom, and from his day to our own the interminable warfare of the sects has retarded progress and brought shame upon Christianity. On the whole, most of us in England and America, in spite of the great reaction in favour of Mediævalism which the last half century has witnessed, in spite of the attitude taken up by a very considerable body of our countrymen who repudiate with scorn the name of Protestant, most of us think that Religious Liberty was worth any sacrifice of unity.   But we cannot help wondering sometimes, when we reflect upon the hostilities which the Reformation has caused—the relig- ious wars, the social strifes, the suicidal competition of sects, the narrowness and the intense individualism to which Protestantism is prone, the multiplication of factions and discords, perpetuated alike in life and in death between brother-men, between friends and kinsmen—whether Goethe was right when he declared that it would have been well for the world if Erasmus and not Luther had guided the Reforming movement.   Nay, furthermore, there are not wanting wise teachers in our midst who warn us that there is a Protestant scholasticism as well as a Catholic.   If Luther, they say, with his dogma of Justification by-Faith, and Calvin with his dogma of Predestination, have triumphed in the past, the future belongs to Erasmus, who sought to diminish dogma, who insisted on the final supremacy of Reason, and strove hard to draw man- kind from the discussion of insoluble mysteries to practical piety and the imitation of Christ.   Certainly if one may judge by the present tone of theology—if, still more, we inquire into the beliefs of average educated English laymen, we shall be forced to the conclusion that the world is becoming, as it once was before, *Erasmian*.   In any case, a pathetic interest attaches to the vain attempts of great and good men like More and Erasmus to preserve the continuity of History, and to hand down to posterity, reformed but not destroyed, the Church of Western Christendom.

There is not much difficulty in indicating the characteristics of this trio of Reformers and their relations to each other.   Colet is primarily a preacher and theologian.   Erasmus, once a monk, is essentially a scholar and man of letters.   More, by profession a lawyer and a statesman, is the original thinker and daring speculator, with gifts of genius far exceeding those of his two friends.   We know least about Colet; but it seems probable that Erasmus derived much of his theology from him, and More many of his ideas on politics and society.   Colet, though born in the same year as Erasmus, 1466, is acknowledged by him as his master and teacher; but the genius and intellectual power of More seem to have altogether neutralized his twelve years of inferiority in age. To mark the epoch it may be well to bear in mind that when Colet was born, the Wars of the Roses were still distracting England, and that when he died Luther was just about to break with Rome. We have to deal with the age of the Medici and the Borgias, of Richard III. and Henry VIII., of Columbus and Savonarola, of Luther and Ignatius Loyola, of Thomas Cromwell and Machiavelli—an age you will remember, distinguished beyond most others by its portentous wickedness and moral degradation.

John Colet was the son of Sir Henry Colet, a rich and prosperous mercer who became Lord Mayor of London in the year following the battle of Bosworth. He was the first-born of a large family of twenty-one sons and daughters, none of whom save himself lived beyond childhood. He was educated at one of the few famous schools which London then possessed, S. Anthony's, where one may hope there was more instruction and less flogging than was usual in fifteenth-century schools, which, if Erasmus may be trusted, stood as much in need of reform as any institutions of Christendom. "At the present time," he writes in one of his tracts, "all public instruction has passed into the hands of schoolmasters. And though there ought to have been the greatest care in appointing them, those assigned to the post are, as a rule, a shabby, broken-down set of men, sometimes hardly in their senses. So mean the place, so miserable the pittance, you would say the pigs were being reared there, and not that respectable people's children were being taught." History commemorates Dean Colet's name if for nothing else, for this, that before he died he had begun a revolution in middle-class education of which the beneficial results have endured to our own day.

At the age of seventeen he was a student at Oxford; and it is worth our while perhaps to try to realize what the University was like when Richard III. was king, in the last dying epoch of the Middle Ages. Outwardly it was not at all the Oxford of to-day. John Colet as he journeyed from London would pass over no beautiful

many-arched Magdalen bridge.   That, of course, is a mere
creature of yesterday, barely a hundred and ten years old. He would
see Magdalen but without its tower, of which the first stone was not
laid until 1492, and without its groves, which date from the reign
of Elizabeth.   Half of the colleges which are familiar to us were
then absent.   Christ Church, the magnificent creation of Wolsey,
did not come into existence until 1525.   There was no Corpus,
no Brasenose, no S. John's or Trinity, still less such modern .
growths as Wadham and Worcester.   But Colet would know
Merton and Balliol, the two oldest foundations; and the venerable University College, which is not so venerable, however, as
some persons would have us believe.   He would see Queen's and
New College, Exeter, Oriel, Lincoln and All Souls.   The Bod-
leian Library as we know it belongs of course to a later century, but
the Divinity School, when Colet arrived in Oxford, was fresh from
the hands of Duke Humphrey of Gloucester's workmen; and it is
a safe conjecture that he must often have listened there, probably
not without scorn and anger, to the disputations of scholastic
divines and the wordy warfare of Thomists and Scotists.   The chief
feature, however, of mediæval Oxford was the existence of numer- .
ous establishments belonging to the monastic orders.   It was still
almost a city of monks and friars.   The Benedictines had their
hostels on the site of Worcester; the Dominicans had their home
in S. Ebbe's; Carmelites, Minorites, and Cistercians thronged the
streets; S. Frideswide's nunnery had given place to a priory of
Augustinians, who also possessed a College for their student
canons near New Inn Lane, where Erasmus was hospitably
received when he first came to Oxford in 1498.

As to the life of the students, what most strikes us is their
poverty and the hardships of their lot.   Oxford was not then the
exclusive possession of a small wealthy class.   It was the home of
poor students, who lived on hard fare, in squalid tenements, needing constantly the attention of rat-catchers in their straw-littered
dormitories, forced from time to time to deposit in pawn in the
University chests some article of value in order to obtain a meal,
possessing few books and scanty furniture, finding almost their
sole means of recreation and athletic exercise in street brawls with

townsmen, living chiefly by mendicancy. Mediæval poems constantly allude to the begging of undergraduates on their way to the University, and late in the reign of Henry VIII. measures were taken to keep the practice within bounds. " Be it enacted," says a statute of the realm, " that scholars of the Universities of Oxford and Cambridge that go about begging, not being authorized under the seal of the said Universities by the Chancellor or Vice-Chancellor of the same, shall be punished as is before rehearsed of sturdy beggars and vagabonds."

We need not, however, despise these mediæval students. Their poverty may perhaps raise in our minds certain inconvenient doubts as to whether the endowments of the ancient Universities have not been diverted in many cases from the classes for whom they were originally intended and who stand most in need of them. At any rate, we may be sure that the zeal for learning displayed by those tattered gownsmen of the Middle Ages, who often as not begged their food, was at least as great as that displayed by their modern successors. Perhaps they cared for knowledge more than we do. "In the chilly squalor of uncarpeted aad unwarmed chambers," says a recent historian of Oxford, the Warden of Merton, "by the light of narrow and unglazed casements, or the gleam of flickering oil-lamps, poring over dusky manuscripts hardly to be deciphered by modern eyesight, men of humble birth, and dependent on charity for a bare subsistence, but with a noble self-confidence transcending that of Bacon and Newton, thought out and copied out those subtle masterpieces of mediæval lore, purporting to unveil the hidden laws of Nature as well as the dark counsels of Providence and the secrets of human destiny."

What exactly Colet studied when he came to Oxford is a little difficult to explain, for the Revival of Learning has placed an impassable gulf between the knowledge of that day and of ours. The jargon of the Schoolmen has become unintelligible to us. We can understand the studies of a Roger Ascham or a Queen Elizabeth—Homer and Demosthenes and the Greek Testament, —for to a large extent our training is the same ; but which of us, I wonder, can boast of an intimate acquaintance with the books which Colet must have read for his degree,—Priscian's Grammar, the treatises of Boethius on Arithmetic and Music, the "Nova Rhetorica" of Cicero, the "De Interpretatione" of Aristotle? There is only one work, in fact, on the list which is common to the educational training of that day and our own, and this is Euclid's Elements. When Colet arrived in Oxford the University had not emerged from the intellectual mists of the Middle Ages. In Italy the Revival of Learning had been in full progress for half a century or more, but England was still practically untouched by it. Exiles from Constantinople as early as 1441 had lectured in Florence on the Greek classics. Cosimo de Medici, shortly before his death in 1464, had founded the Platonic Academy; but barbarian England lagged behind, and it is extremely doubtful whether, when Colet first came to Oxford, there was a man in the University,—Master, Doctor, or Vice-Chancellor,—who could translate Greek into English. We can have no more striking illustration of the backwardness of England in culture and civilization than the fact that a brother of the Black Prince once banqueted with Petrarch, the first of the Italian Humanists, in the palace of Galeazzo Visconti; that is to say, while England was still feudal and mediæval, Italy, as Mr. J. H. Symonds tells us, "socially and mentally, had entered upon the modern era."

Already, however, a stray scholar or two from Oxford had found his way to the Italian Universities and had imbibed the gifts of that New Learning which was destined so quickly to transform the life of Europe. Amongst the first of these was Thomas Linacre, a Fellow of All Souls, the celebrated founder of the College of Physicians, who, about the same time when Colet arrived in Oxford, was receiving the highest education the world could give, in company with Lorenzo de Medici's children at Florence. To Florence also was drawn, as to the source of knowledge and scholarship, another Oxford Fellow, William Grocyn, who studied under the great Italian humanist Politian, and returning here, publicly taught the Greek language, much to the pain of certain orthodox divines who regarded it as a Pagan and heretical tongue. To William Grocyn belongs the credit of having opened the treasures of the New Learning to two of the most famous scholars of the next generation, Erasmus and Sir Thomas More.

The third channel of communication between Italy and England was Colet himself. He left Oxford in 1494, and spent the next two years in Italy "like a merchant," as Erasmus writes, "seeking goodly pearls." Unfortunately, we have no detailed information regarding his life in Italy, nor do we know absolutely that he visited Florence. The indirect evidence that he did so, nevertheless, seems altogether convincing. The intellectual predominance of Florence was at this period so marked that no traveling scholar in search of knowledge could possibly have avoided the fair city on the Arno where the greatest scholars and men of letters and artists of the world had their home. Colet's sermons and lectures bear the clearest marks of the influence of three men, Marsilio Ficino, Pico della Mirandola, and Girolamo Savonarola, all Florentines, If Colet ever reached Florence at all, and it is incredible that he did not, he must have come directly into contact with the Prior of San Marco, at that time the central figure in Florence. It is allowable to think of the young Oxford student listening, with the artists Botticelli and Michel Angelo, with historians like Machiavelli and Guicciardini, with the most learned scholars and the humblest poor of Florence, to the, fiery words of Italy's most powerful preacher as he stood beneath the dome of Brunelleschi, denouncing the corruptions of the Church and the evil lives of Popes and prelates. This, of course, is mere guess work. But at any rate it is beyond doubt that John Colet, first leader of the English Renaissance, whether or not he ever saw Savonarola, is Savonarola's spiritual disciple. You cannot read the sermons of the two men without being struck by their close and intimate resemblance. Their principles are identical—reform without revolution, loyalty to the idea of the Catholic Church, unrelenting warfare alike against worldly ecclesiastics and selfish, ambitious tyrants, devotion to the Scriptures, Puritan morality.

The only historical evidence that we possess regarding this Italian visit of Colet's is contained in the words of Erasmus. "Colet devoted himself," he says, " at this time entirely to the

study of the sacred writers." The sentence is significant, and
indicates the course which the Revival of Letters was to take
in Germany and England, where Renaissance meant Reformation—not a return to Paganism, but a return to Scriptural
Christianity. We should naturally have expected that in the
chosen home of the Classical Revival, Colet would have studied
chiefly, not S. Paul, but Plato and Cicero. Perhaps if he had
reached Italy five years earlier, when Lorenzo de Medici was
alive, when the enthusiasm for ancient civilization was at its
height, when Marsilio Ficino, it was said, kept a lamp burning
before the bust of Plato as well as before the image of the Virgin,
he too might have imbibed the sympathies of the Italian
Humanists. But he came to Italy during the epoch of the
reaction. Lorenzo was dead. Savonarola was all-powerful. The
reign of Pagan license was over for the time. Scorn was being
cast by the fervid monk upon all attempts to exalt the ancient
philosophers above the Christian writers as guides of life. The
Bible, and the Bible only, was preached from Savonarola's pulpit.
And so it came about that when Colet returned to Oxford in
1496, fresh from contact with Italian learning, he began at once
to lecture, not upon the works of any classical author, but upon
S. Paul's Epistle to the Romans. His lectures mark an era in the
history of religious thought in England. Colet was an unauthor-
ized teacher and had taken no degree in Divinity, but his fresh and
original treatment of the Scriptures drew all Oxford, abbots and
heads of houses included, to his lecture rooms. He was fiercely
in earnest, and disdained to receive fees from his hearers. "The
race for professorships and fees," he told Erasmus, "spoilt everything, and adulterated the purity of all branches of learning."

By a fortunate accident, the manuscripts of these lectures have
been preserved at Cambridge, and we can know accurately what
Colet's religious position was. In the first place, he was the
deadly foe of the Schoolmen and their absurd, complicated
methods of Scriptural interpretation. He did not, as some are
inclined to do in modern times, underrate the intellectual power
of such masters of subtle reasoning as S. Thomas Aquinas; but
his Italian studies had brought him face to face with the New

Testament, and the Renaissance spirit of free thought had made
him a rebel against a system of complicated beliefs and dogmatic
teachings resting upon no surer basis than a false and artificial
.Scriptural interpretation. The Schoolmen treated the Bible as
a mere arsenal of texts. They despised its plain and literal
meaning, and insisted on finding types and allegories in the
simplest details. "They divide the Scripture," says William
Tyndale, "into four senses—the literal, tropological, allegorical,
and anagogical : the literal sense has become nothing at all.
Twenty doctors expound one text twenty ways, and with an
antitheme of half an inch some of them draw a thread of nine
days long. They not only say that the literal sense profiteth
nothing, but also that it is noisome and hurtful and killeth the
soul. And this they prove by a text of Paul : 'The letter killeth,
but the spirit giveth life.' Lo ! they say, the literal sense killeth,
but the spirit giveth life."

Against all this Colet made incessant war. It is his great claim
to our respect that though he lived in the last years of the Middle
Age, though he was a loyal Catholic, he yet rejected the teaching of
the scholastic divines, brushed aside their inventions and traditions,
and went back to the words and life of Christ. He would have
nothing to do with S. Thomas Aquinas and his brief compendium
of doctrines to be believed extending to 1150 huge folio pages,
containing, although the great doctor called his book "milk for
babes," forty-three separate propositions concerning the nature
of God, ten propositions regarding the Creation, forty-five respecting the nature of Man before and after the Fall, and treating as
not unimportant the discussion of such articles of faith as these :
Whether an angel can be in more than one place at one and the
same time ? Whether more angels than one can be in one and the
same place at the same time ? Whether angels have local motion ?
and a thousand similar inanities.

It is no wonder surely that the young Dutch scholar Erasmus,
brought under the influence of the scholastic divines at the
University of Paris, came to distrust theology. He dared not
study it, he said. If he did, he should soon be branded as a
heretic. The time had come when men were to be freed from

mediæval burdens. "Keep firmly to the Bible and the Apostles' Creed," was John Colet's advice to his pupils: "let divines, if they like, dispute about the rest."

We must not suppose, however, that he had entirely freed himself from the theological trammels of his time. Colet, intellectual child of the Renaissance though he was, amazing as was the boldness with which he anticipated many of the conclusions of modern religious thought, had, nevertheless, one foot in the Middle Ages. No Protestant could have poured greater contempt upon image-worship and pilgrimages than he did, but his temper was ascetic and monastic. He had little of the humanist spirit which appears in all the writings of Erasmus and in More's 'Utopia.' The Paganism of the Italian scholars had forced him, as it compelled Savonarola, to adopt narrow and illiberal opinions regarding the classical authors. It does not appear to have been generally noticed that when he founded S. Paul's School, he omitted the study of Cicero and Virgil, Demosthenes and Plato, and enjoined the reading only of such writers as "hath with wisdom joined the pure chaste eloquence," such as the fourth century author, Lactantius, who together with good Latinity combined decent Christian morals. We should be glad to forget that a Reformer so generally broad-minded as Colet once advised his hearers at Oxford: "Those books only ought to be read in which there is a salutary flavour of Christ—in which Christ is set forth for us to feast upon. Do not become readers of philosophers, companions of devils." He was a mediævalist too in his views on marriage, which he regarded as an inferior state, as a concession to human infirmities. When it was objected to him that if his doctrines were adopted by Christians, the race of men would soon become extinct and the Church be left without members, he only pointed to the heathen as materials for grace. If they all became Christians and remained single, then, he thought, the human race would come to an end in a state of sanctity, and so much the better. But, he added, with a touch of caustic humour, there was no fear of such a result. The heathen might be converted to Christianity, but just as fast professing Christians would relapse into practical heathenism.

In these extreme opinions of his, we have Colet at his worst. He is at his best and strongest when he leads the way to a rational interpretation of the Bible. His greatness as a theologian is not to be estimated by his own writings, but by the influence which he exercised over his friends. He taught Erasmus what Erasmus afterwards taught the world. He helped to make More what he was—the boldest thinker and the most perfect man of his generation.

John Colet, however, was greater as a preacher than as a theologian, and it is his work as Dean of S. Paul's which chiefly merits attention. His lectures at Oxford brought him into contact with many who influenced the future life of England; possibly with Wolsey, who in 1498 was a tutor in Magdalen School; possibly with William Tyndale, who was then an undergraduate of Magdalen Hall; certainly with Erasmus, who had been introduced to him in the same year, 1498. But Oxford was still in bonds to the Schoolmen, looked with suspicion upon new movements, and shewed no favour to the young scholar who treated the Bible not as an armoury of texts, but as a literature, as a Divine record indeed, but also as a book to be interpreted like any other book. To the end of his stay in Oxford, Colet was a mere free lance, unhonoured by his University, obliged to wait patiently for an opportunity of advancing those great reforms in Church and State for which he longed.

In the year 1505, the opportunity came, when he was made Dean of S. Paul's by King Henry VII. It was a position of great usefulness but of peculiar difficulty. The Bishop belonged to the school of thought which was passing away, and from the first regarded Colet as little better than a heretic. The Chapter was corrupt, and demoralized by the ceaseless stream of wealth which poured into its coffers from the offerings of the Cathedral. Colet, like Savonarola, thought that those whose duty it was to preach " Blessed are ye poor," had better not possess enormous. revenues and live like princes. He thought that the Church stood in imminent danger of ruin from the worldly lives of prelates, from the abuses and scandals of ecclesiastical administration, which had brought the clergy into universal contempt with honest men.

"How much greediness and appetite of honour and dignity," he boldly told Convocation in 1512, "is nowadays in men of the Church! How run they, yea almost out of breath, from one benefice to another: from the less to the more, from the lower to the higher! Who seeth not this? Who seeing this sorroweth not? Moreover, these that are in the same dignities, the most part of them doth go with so stately a countenance, and with so high looks, that they seem not to be put in the humble bishopric of Christ, but rather in the high lordship and power of the world." Such a man as this was not likely to find the Deanery of S. Paul's in the early sixteenth century a bed of roses, nor did he. Like Abbot Samson of S. Edmund's monastery, in Carlyle's famous sketch, Colet had a sore time of it after his elevation to high office. He attempted to reform his Chapter, and failed. The greed and covetousness of the Canons were inveterate, and Colet's reforming zeal was conquered by their dogged resistance.

He was more successful in making his Cathedral pulpit a centre of influence. For twenty years he had been steadily preparing himself for the work of a preacher, and had studied carefully, as Erasmus tells us, the works of English poets in order that he might speak to the hearts of the people. He had listened, in all probability, to the sermons of Savonarola, and at any rate was animated by the same glowing earnestness and lofty ambition to cleanse the Church and stem the torrent of corruption which threatened to engulf it in disaster. No such preaching as Colet's, it may be safely asserted, had been heard in England for a hundred years. In him the spirit of Hugh of Lincoln, who withstood kings like Richard Lionheart and John Lackland, of Robert Grosseteste, who toiled laboriously to root out abuses and to reform the Church, lived again. Not even Savonarola himself displayed more fearless courage in denouncing powerful offenders and boldly attacking flagrant crimes of princes and prelates. In the year 1512, the Dean of S. Paul's was called upon by Archbishop Warham the firm friend of the New Learning and its advocates, to preach before Convocation, and his sermon, it has been rightly said by Colet's most recent biographer, Mr. Lupton, "marks an epoch in the history of the English Church. More truly than any other single speech or act, it deserves to be called the overture in the great drama of the English Reformation." The Convocation of 1512 was not an inspiring audience for an earnest, pure-hearted Church Reformer to look upon. No wise historical student trusts any longer the partisan histories of the Reformation which our grandfathers received as veracious; but when all allowance has been made for Protestant exaggerations, the case against the pre-Reformation clergy remains overwhelmingly strong. Colet's Convocation audience would contain many prelates of the type of Wolsey, then Dean of Lincoln, and Henry VIII.'s most trusted minister, scheming politicians rather than rulers of the Church, as worldly as Wolsey but without his genius. There would be some, no doubt, of the same stamp as the young boy, shallow-brained, but of noble family, whom Erasmus once declined to cram for a Bishopric; some like the illiterate Bishop whom Sir Thomas More satirized in a stinging epigram, one of the ignorant opponents of the Revival of Letters, who defended the allegorical interpretations of the Schoolmen by the usual text, "The letter killeth, but the spirit giveth life," and drew down upon himself More's laughing retort that he was "too illiterate for any letters to have killed him, and if they had, he had no spirit to bring him to life again." Half the prelates whom Colet had to address had received their promotion, not through any especial holiness of life or fitness for their offices, but purely on account of political services rendered to the crown. Not a few of the Bishops were foreigners and lived abroad. Some were thoroughly bad men, like James Stanley, a connection of the Royal family, and a member of a noble house, who in 1506 was pitchforked into a Bishopric, and soon became notorious throughout England for the open immorality of his life. The Convocation of 1512, it is clear, was not likely to receive with acclamation the reforming projects of a Puritan like John Colet. It had met together to arrange stronger measures for the extirpation of heretics, and Colet told his hearers to their faces that the most pernicious heresy of all was the evil and depraved lives of the clergy. His opening words struck the keynote of his sermon. "You are come together to-day, fathers and right wise men, to hold a council. I wish that, mindful of your name and profession,

ye would consider of the reformation of ecclesiastical affairs; for
never was it more necessary, and never did the state of the Church
more need your endeavours.   For the Church, the spouse of Christ,
which He wished to be without spot or wrinkle, is become foul
and deformed."

The distinguishing mark of the reforming programme of Colet
and the Oxford Reformers was that it aimed at changes in life and
practice, not in doctrine.   Colet has no word to say against Papal
Supremacy or the Mass, and there need be no doubt that if he had
lived he would have been found by the side of Thomas More,
contending hotly against Luther.   But he thunders against the
worldliness and pride, the covetousness and luxury and secular occu-
pations of the prelates of his day.   " Magistracy in the Church,"
he tells dignitaries like Wolsey, " is nothing else than humble
service.   He who is chief, let him be the servant of all."   In the
ears of scandalous persons like James Stanley, Bishop of Ely, he
describes with unheard-of plainness of speech the immoral lives of
ecclesiastics.   "They give themselves up to feasting and ban-
queting," he says : "spend themselves in vain babbling, take part
in sports and plays, devote themselves to hunting and hawking ;
are drowned in the delights of this world."   Worst of all the corruptions of the time, however, Colet ranks the race for wealth
which had infected his order.   " What else in these days," he asks
the astonished Convocation, " do we seek for in the Church than
rich benefices and promotions?   In these same promotions, what
else do we count upon but their fruits and revenues?   We rush
after them with such eagerness, that we care not how many and
what duties or how great benefices we take, if only they have great
revenues.   O Covetousness!   Paul rightly called thee the root of
all evil.   From thee comes all this piling-up of benefices one on the
top of the other ; from thee quarrels about tithes, about offerings,
about mortuaries, about ecclesiastical right and title, for which we
fight as for our very lives. Why should I mention the rest? Every
corruption, all the ruin of the Church, all the scandals of the world,
come from the covetousness of priests."

And then the fiery Dean of S. Paul's went on to propose his
remedies.   No new laws were wanted, he said.   Let the Bishops

reform their lives. Let the ecclesiastical courts, which enabled the clergy to prey upon the laity, be transformed. Let residence be enforced, and wicked and ignorant persons be no longer admitted to holy orders. Let the rulers of the Church, instead of posing as princes and statesmen, watch over their flocks, hear the causes of the poor, sustain the fatherless, and spend their lives in works of piety.

Finally, Colet warned the Convocation, as though foreseeing the catastrophe which was impending, that the need for reform was urgent. "Consider the miserable state and condition of the Church," he concluded, "and bend your whole minds to its Reformation. Suffer not, fathers, suffer not this so illustrious assembly to break up without result. Suffer not this your congregation to slip by for nothing. Ye have indeed often been assembled. But (if by your leave I may speak the truth) I see not what fruit has as yet resulted from assemblies of this kind."

Colet might as well have preached to the winds. The only result of the sermon seems to have been that henceforth the Dean of S. Paul's was a marked man. Before the year was out a charge of heresy was brought against him by his own Bishop, Fitzjames of London, who had been hostile to him from the first. The accusations were somewhat frivolous. The first was that he had said that images were not to be worshipped; the second, that he had denied that the command to Peter, "Feed my lambs," had anything to do with Episcopal hospitality, Saint Peter having possessed no Episcopal revenues; the third, that he had reflected upon his Bishop for his habit of reading his sermons. Colet made no reply to such nonsense, and Archbishop Warham indignantly rejected the charges.

Later on, Colet's enemies found a more serious accusation against him. It was an age of unjust and selfish wars, waged mainly to satisfy the vanity or ambition of kings. In 1513, Henry VIII. had engaged in one of these, and Colet, who hated all war with passionate hatred, being called upon to preach a Good Friday sermon before the King and his Court, with reckless boldness, seized the occasion to denounce the war-fever of his time. "He shewed," says Erasmus, "that when wicked men, out of hatred and ambition, fought with and destroyed one another, they fought under the banner not of Christ but of the devil. He shewed further, how hard a thing it is to die a Christian death on the field of battle: how few undertake a war except from hatred or ambition ; and urged, in conclusion, that instead of imitating the Cæsars and Alexanders, the Christian ought rather to follow the example of Christ his prince."

The zeal of Henry's soldiers had been damped by Colet's earnest invective, and immediately after the sermon he was summoned to an interview with the King. His enemies openly rejoiced, and expected his speedy downfall. Henry VIII., however, was still generous and noble, and he treated Colet with the greatest kindness. "Let every one have his own doctor," he said to his courtiers after the interview, "and let every one favor his own; this man is the doctor for me." "And so," concludes Erasmus in his account of the matter, "certain wolves departed, open-mouthed as the saying is, nor did any one from that day forward venture to molest Colet."

He lived six years after this: long enough to see his teaching carried forward and developed by Erasmus in his ' New Testament,' and by Sir Thomas More in the ' Utopia' : long enough also to see the first begginnings of that second Reforming movement which was destined to obscure and destroy his own. He died in 1519, " to the great grief of the whole people," as his epitaph relates, " by whom, for his integrity of life and divine gift of preaching, he was the most beloved of all his time."

That part of Dean Colet's work for England which met with most immediate success, and was distinctively his own, as compared with results which were due to his disciples Erasmus and More, was his reform of education and the foundation of S. Paul's School in London. In an age when schools in England were for the most part barbarous and cruel, antiquated in method, devoted to barren and useless studies, he founded a great institution which became soon a veritable home of the New Learning, supplied a model for the succeeding foundations of the Tudor epoch, produced John Milton in the seventeenth century, and at the present date sends out probably a greater number of famous classical scholars than any other school in England. Colet was drawn to this work partly by his hatred of Scholasticism and his zeal for the Revival of Letters, partly by his love of children. He lavished on S. Paul's property equivalent to £40,000 of our money, and watched over its welfare with unremitting care. He was perhaps even more anxious that his students should be good men than great scholars, and would cordially have accepted the saying of Ruskin in our own time, "Education does not mean teaching people to know what they do not know. It means teaching them to behave as they do not behave." "My intent by this school," he says in the statutes, "is specially to increase the knowledge and worshipping of God and our Lord Christ Jesus, and good Christian life and manners in the children." The New Learning, however, held a predominant place in Colet's new scheme. Greek was taught at S. Paul's, greatly to the indignation of Bishop Fitzjames and other advocates of the studies that were passing away, who denounced Colet's school as a dangerous and heretical institution. The best men of the Revival, on the other hand, aided him in his work. The first High-master of the school was William Lilly, a brilliant scholar, the companion of More, who had traveled in Greece and had shared with Grocyn and Linacre the honor of being the first to bring back to England knowledge of the Greek language. Erasmus himself wrote grammars and text-books for Colet's students. Both he and More were quick to see the importance of the new departure, and it was indeed a movement of far-reaching consequences. "The grammar schools of Edward the Sixth and of Elizabeth," says J. R. Green, "in a word, the system of middle-class education which by the close of the century had changed the very face of England, were the direct results of Colet's foundation of S. Paul's." As for the spirit in which he entered upon his work, the best illustration of it is to be found in the preface to the Accidence which he wrote for his scholars, which remains as a testimony to the gentle, tender nature of one who has been called "the first of the Puritans," who with all his severity "took a delight," as Erasmus says, "in the purity and simplicity of nature that is in children." "I have been willing," Colet writes in the introduction to his book, "to speak the things often before spoken in such manner as gladly young beginners and tender wits might take and conceive. Wherefore, I pray you, all little babies, all little children, learn gladly this little treatise, and commend it diligently unto your memories. Trusting of this beginning that ye shall proceed and grow to perfect literature, and come at last to be great clerks. And lift up your little white hands for me which prayeth for you to God: to whom be all honour and imperial majesty and glory. Amen."

And there we must take leave of Dean Colet. "You would not hesitate," wrote Erasmus to a friend when he died, "to inscribe the name of this man in the roll of saints although uncanonised by the Pope." "For generations," wrote More, "we have not had amongst us any one man more learned or holy."

LECTURE II.

𝕰𝖗𝖆𝖘𝖒𝖚𝖘.

" Erasmus was in truth, in his own age, the great Apostle of common-sense and of rational religion. He did not care for dogma; and accordingly the dogmas of Rome, which had the consent of the Christian world, were in his eyes preferable to the dogmas of Protestantism, which destroyed the unity of the Church and threatened to open the way for every sort of extravagance. What he did care for was practical Christianity, and that he advocated with an earnestness and eloquence, and an unwearied devotion, which have perhaps never been surpassed. Peace, good-will, justice, righteousness, charity,—in pleading the cause of these virtues he knew neither fear nor favor. From the beginning to the end of his career he remained true to the great purpose of his life, which was to fight the battle of sound learning and plain common-sense against the powers of ignorance and superstition, and amid all the convulsions of that period he never once lost his mental balance."—R. B. DRUMMOND.

" He was brilliantly gifted. His industry never tired. His intellect was true to itself; and no worldly motives ever tempted him into insincerity. He was even far braver than he professed to be. Had he been brought to the trial, he would have borne it better than many a man who boasted louder of his courage."—J. A. FROUDE.

" The one name in which the classical revival of Germany is summed up, is that of Erasmus. He is the typical northern scholar. No contemporary Italian humanist had so great a reputation: he was recognized on both sides of the Alps as the literary chief of Europe."—Hibbert Lectures for 1883.

" A man with many faults, many weaknesses, with much vanity, with a want of independence of character; faults surely venial considering the circumstances of his birth, his loneliness in the world, his want of natural friends, and even of country, and his physical infirmities: but a man who in the great period of dawning intellect, stood forth the foremost; who in the scholar never forgot the Christian; whose avowed object it was to associate the cultivation of letters with a simpler Christianity, a Christianity of life as of doctrine; who in influence at least was the greatest of the ' Reformers before the Reformation.' "—DEAN MILMAN.

THE difficulty which had to be met in speaking of the life of Dean Colet was the scantiness of the materials which have come down to us. The difficulty in the case of Erasmus is the extreme abundance of materials and the boundless number of interesting facts from which one has to select. I need hardly say that of these three Oxford Reformers, Erasmus, both in his own lifetime and since, has occupied by far the chief place in the world's estimation. His life has been written many times, though never perhaps in a manner worthy of the great scholar; but no English writer has thought it worth while to give us a complete and adequate biography of Sir Thomas More. Colet and More, however, are mainly interesting to Englishmen. Erasmus belongs to Europe. He is a cosmopolitan, and no single country can claim exclusive possession of him. Holland gave him birth. France gave him éducation. England was generous to him when poor and unknown, and he loved her well, far better than his own country—"bread-and-butter land," as he scornfully termed it. Italy opened out to him the treasures of antiquity and enabled him to lead the Renaissance movement North of the Alps. Germany in the person of Charles V. courted him. Switzerland, when the Lutheran struggle grew hot and furious, afforded him a secure retreat during his later years. He wrote all his works in Latin, the common language of all educated Europeans in his time, and despised modern tongues, "uncouth, barbarous dialects," as they appeared to him. His position as chief amongst the aristocracy of scholars turned the eyes of the learned upon him. His own industry in letter-writing and his genial egotism combined to make his personality better known than that of any other man in Western Christendom.　He was many-sided, and the interest of his life is almost inexhaustible.　In an hour's space it will be hard to convey any adequate idea of his amazing activity as a thinker and man of letters, of his friendships and his quarrels, of his writing, of his unbounded influence over the educated men of his age.

The youth of Erasmus is a tragic history which ought to incline us to a merciful judgment of his faults.　The pitiful tale is no doubt familiar to most of you from the dramatic presentment of it in tolerably faithful details in Charles Reade's novel, 'The Cloister and the Hearth.'　It is a terrible record of the suffering and the evil which the supplanting of God's laws of human affection by man's monastic theories too often caused during the Middle Ages.

Erasmus was the base-born son of a youth whom persecution and diabolical fraud on the part of his relations forced into the monastic life which he abhorred.　This youth, Gerard, was the ninth son of a respectable poor tradesman who lived at Tergou in Holland.　Religious superstition induced his parents to believe that they owed one child to God, that is, to the monks.　This, added to the pressure of a hard struggle for existence, made them resolve to consecrate Gerard, the wittiest and ablest of their sons, to the service of the Church.　Gerard, however, was utterly unwilling.　The thought of a monastery was hateful to him, and morever he had given his heart to a young girl named Margaret, daughter of a physician at Sevenbergen.　They were plighted, but never married.　Gerard was pursued by his family with unrelenting persecution, and at last, in 1466, after Margaret had given birth at Rotterdam to the child who afterwards became famous under the name of Erasmus, he came to a final rupture with his parents and fled to Rome, where he gained success as a skillful copyist of manuscripts.　His ability was great, and he seemed likely to rise from this occupation to scholarship and a career as a lawyer, when a treacherous fraud on the part of his parents suddenly changed his whole life.　They had never given up their intention that he should become a monk, and inasmuch as Gerard's love for Margaret stood in the way, they stooped to the basest artifice and sent him word that she was dead. In his despair he entered a monastery and took the vows. Then soon afterwards returning to his own country, he found Margaret alive and well. His love for her had never wavered, but he was now a priest, sworn to a celibate life, and, with heroic conscientiousness, he surrendered his hopes of happiness and remained faithful to his priestly vows until the day of his death. The hapless monk and the ill-fated Margaret found now their one consolation in caring for the two children who had been born to them. Gerard sent his little Erasmus to the famous school of Deventer, and there Margaret, hearing that the town was stricken by the plague and hastening to save her son, caught the infection and died. Gerard, not yet forty years old, broken-hearted, soon followed her to the grave, and at thirteen Erasmus was left an orphan in the charge of cruel and unscrupulous guardians.

The second chapter in his life is no less gloomy and tragic. The curse of enforced monasticism darkened his youth as it had his father's. Gerard had been entrapped into the priesthood by a cunning falsehood; his son was inveigled into a monastery by treachery concealed under the guise of friendship. All in vain, his guardian, Peter Winckel, having embezzled his little property, endeavored, first by persuasion, then by threats and fears, to induce the lad to become a monk. Already at fifteen Erasmus longed for a scholar's life. "From the very first," says Mark Pattison, "the love of letters was the one ruling motive of his career." He might have resisted successfully the determination of his guardians to force him into a convent, but for the advice of a false friend, Cornelius Werden, who had himself joined a monastery at Stein, and who drew for him attractive pictures of the cultured leisure, the boundless opportunities for quiet study, the serene piety, which were to be found with the monks. His scruples were removed, and in the year 1486, at the age of nineteen, he entered upon his probation. For a while all went well. He was allowed to study as he chose, and monastic life was made easy for him. But long before the time arrived for taking the final step, disenchantment came. He found himself surrounded by idle, ignorant, and for the most part vicious men. The life of the monks, once pure and holy, had reached its worst degradation in the 15th century. "A monk's holy obedience," Erasmus wrote in latter years, "consists in—what? In leading an honest, chaste, and sober life? Not the least. In acquiring learning, in study, and industry? Still less. A monk may be a glutton, a drunkard, an ignorant, stupid, malignant, envious, bad man, but he has broken no vow, he is within his holy obedience. He has only to be the slave of a superior as bad as himself, and he is an excellent brother." Even had it been otherwise, had culture prevailed instead of intense ignorance and coarseness, had piety and good works existed instead of laziness and gluttony and drinking bouts intermingled with outward observances and fastings, Erasmus knew himself to be unfitted for the monastic career. His health was feeble, his constitution liable to terrible disease. Frequent fasting was an impossibility to him. Fish, the staple food of the monastery, he could not eat. His heart, as he once said, was Catholic, but his stomach was Protestant. Like most eager students he found sleep difficult, and once aroused he could not sleep again. As the day drew near when he must take the final step, his dislike to the monastic existence became intensified. He appealed to his guardians. He threw himself upon the humanity of the monks. "Had they been," he wrote afterwards, "good, Christian, religious men, they would have known how unfit I was for their life. I was neither made for them nor they for me." The monks, however, would show him no mercy. They urged upon him that he had put his hand to the plow and must not turn back. It would be a sin before Heaven, and he would be infamous in the sight of all men, if he now withdrew. They reminded him of the stigma and the excommunication, social and religious, which awaited the apostate monk. His scruples, they assured him, were mere devices of Satan, which must be resisted and conquered. At last the poor lad, coaxed, threatened, denounced, deserted by his guardians, uncared for by his kinsmen, gave way and took the vows. Six years he spent in the monastery of Stein, not altogether unprofitably perhaps as regards his studies, for even there his indomitable love of learning enabled him to become one of the most brilliant Latin scholars of the time, but not without evil effects on his moral character, which he himself acknowledged with remorse in latter life. At the end of six years, his deliverance came, and the most painful chapter in his history closed. The Bishop of Cambray, having hopes of being made a Cardinal at Rome, and needing a secretary who could write for him with elegant Latinity, chose Erasmus for the post; but about the year 1492, having no further need of his services, he set him free and aided him in becoming a student at the University of Paris, then the chief centre of higher education on this side of the Alps, thronged by 10,000 students, mostly young, mostly poor. Paris, however, did little for Erasmus. Scholastic studies chiefly prevailed, and the New Learning of Italy had few adherents. There was indeed a Professor of Greek, George Hermonymus of Sparta, but he was incompetent, and as Erasmus said, "could not have taught if he would, and would not if he could." Without Greek, however, Erasmus felt that he was nothing. He longed for Italy, but was too miserably poor to afford the journey. His poverty, indeed, exposed him at Paris to the greatest hardships. At the College of Montaigu, to which he belonged, the lodgings were filthy and pestilential, the food loathsome, the treatment barbarous and cruel. Erasmus declares that in this horrible place he had seen many students of high promise struck down by blindness, leprosy, and the plague. "I brought away from my College at Paris," he says of himself, "nothing but a broken constitution and plenty of vermin."

No hardships, however, could daunt the young scholar's enthusiasm for learning. Disappointed in his hope of Italy, he made his way to Oxford. Already he made his mark as a brilliant member of the Republic of Letters, and was beginning to gather round him a circle of faithful and attached friends. Amongst these was his pupil, the rich English nobleman, Lord Mountjoy, by whose generosity he was enabled to come to Oxford, and who is entitled to the largest share of credit in aiding Erasmus to become the greatest scholar of his time.

England received him with open arms, and at Oxford he soon became the intimate friend of John Colet, Grocyn and Linacre, the opponents of the old scholastic theology, the first founders of the reformed learning in England. Here at last he received from

William Grocyn that knowledge of the Greek language which he
had so long desired in vain, giving to the historian, Edmund
Gibbon, thereby the opportunity of uttering that malicious half-
truth of his, that "Erasmus learnt Greek at Oxford and taught
it at Cambridge." Without falling a victim to a puerile patriot-
ism for one's own university, it may be permitted, perhaps, to
Oxford men to be proud that it was hither in the year 1498 that
Erasmus bent his steps to procure that new learning by whose
aid he afterwards so powerfully influenced the thought of
Europe.

Oxford gave him something more than mere knowledge of
Greek. His friendship with Colet was of immense advantage to
Erasmus in determining the aims of his life, and in moderating
the Bohemian tendencies of the witty Paris student's nature.
Intellectually, when he arrived in Oxford, he was still in bondage
to the Schoolmen. It was Colet who set him free and taught him
that simpler, more reasonable Christianity which it was the work
of his life to expound to the world.

This first visit to England brought him into contact with his
future life-long friend, Thomas More, the brilliant student whom
John Colet proclaimed to be the one solitary genius whom England
at this time possessed. How or when they first became acquainted
we do not know; but everybody, I suppose, has heard the famous
story related by one of More's biographers, that these two scholars,
whose fame was already known to each other, met accidentally at
the Lord Mayor's table in London. Soon the strangers were
involved in a furious argument, Erasmus, after his custom, abusing
the monks and clergy, More with great skill and ready wit
defending them. Erasmus had the worst of it, and at last it
dawned upon him that this quick-witted antagonist must be the
young genius whose praises John Colet had sung to him. "Aut
tu es Morus aut nullus," he suddenly exclaimed, and was met by
More's ready retort, "Aut tu es Erasmus aut diabolus."

The story may be apocryphal, though Mr. Seebohm, in his
excellent book on the Oxford Reformers, seems to countenance it.
What is certain is that from the year 1498 onward, Colet,
Erasmus, and More are bound together not only by a close

personal friendship, but also by community of aims and almost identical views on the great problems of their time.

Naturally enough, with such friends, Erasmus grew attached to England. " I am not a native of Britain," he once wrote to King Henry VIII., " and yet when I consider how many years I have lived in that country, how many patrons, how many excellent and sincere friends I owe to it, I have as hearty a love and esteem for it as if I had drawn my first breath in it." There was nothing in England he disliked, except the beer! He was surprised, but not displeased, by the custom of the English ladies of according a hearty salute of the lips to all stranger-guests when welcoming them or bidding farewell. A native of Holland, he found our climate endurable. It was as delightful as it was healthy, he reported to his friends. As for the English folk, they were delightful too, only he adds by way of warning, " You must always behave modestly, and not be too free in expressing your dislike of anything which you may see in this country. For the English people are, not without reason, lovers of their native land." England, moreover, in his views was by no means the barbarian and uncultured clime its enemies depicted. "I have found here," he says, "so much polish and learning—not showy, shallow learning, but profound and exact, both in Latin and Greek—that now I hardly care much about going to Italy at all, except for the sake of having been there. When I listen to my friend Colet, it seems to me like listening to Plato himself. In Grocyn, who does not admire the wide range of his knowledge? What could be more searching, deep and refined than the judgment of Linacre? Whenever did nature mould a character more gentle, endearing and happy than Thomas More's?"

If John Colet could have had his way, Erasmus would never have left England. He saw in him a splendid intellect, and the fittest instrument for carrying on the work which he had begun. He entreated him to remain at Oxford, to aid in getting rid of the Scholastic theology which had obscured the Christian Gospel, to do for the Old Testament what he himself was endeavouring to do for St. Paul's Epistles. Erasmus refused. He was thirty-three years old, and had been a student all his life, but he counted himself a mere tyro in scholarship and longed for the opportunities which, after all, only Italy could give. Some day, he told Colet, when he had matured his powers. he would help him in his great work. In January, 1500, the restless scholar, panting for new knowledge, left England for Italy.

Henceforth for fifteen years his history is a record of wanderings from University to University, of hard struggles caused by insufficient means, of gradual conquest of the whole realm of knowledge as it then existed, of daily increasing reputation, of amazing literary activity, of final triumph as the leading man of letters in Europe, courted by Popes and Emperors and Kings. It is almost bewildering to follow him in his wanderings from England to France, from France to Holland, from Holland to Italy, from Italy back to England. In 1500, after leaving Oxford, he had intended to make his way beyond the Alps, but the English custom-house officials robbed him of his money, and he was obliged to betake himself to Paris and earn a few pounds by the publication of his first important book, his 'Adagia,' or collection of classical proverbs. Poor, and often in ill health, his enthusiasm for learning never abated, and it is difficult not to feel intense admiration for his heroic struggle against disease and poverty and gloom. "As soon as I get money," he writes at this time, "I shall buy Greek books, and then I shall buy some clothes." Not till 1505 did he realize the dream of his life and visit Italy, and even then he met with disappointment. The golden age of the Renaissance was over. Instead of a peaceful land of culture and civilization, he found Italy distracted by war. The reigning Pope was Julius II.,Michael Angelo's Julius,who was never happy except at the head of an army, and who was ready to deluge Italy with blood if he might thereby enlarge the temporal dominion of the Papacy. Erasmus, the consistent, determined, unflinching denouncer of war, was brought face to face in the streets of Bologna with a Vicar of Christ, arrayed in jackboots and military attire, triumphing at the head of a mercenary army of scoundrels and banditti over conquered foes. What Leo X. and Rome did for Luther, Julius II. and Bologna did for Erasmus. He remained all his life faithful to the idea of Papal Supremacy, but he did not hesitate to denounce in the plainest language such popes as Alexander VI., Julius II., and Leo X. While Julius was still alive he dared to use, in a satire which was read all over Europe, such words as these. "Though war is so cruel," he wrote, "that it becomes wild beasts rather than men, so pestilential that it brings in its train a universal dissolution of manners, so impious that it has no connection with Christ, so unjust that it is usually carried on best by the worst robbers; yet, neglecting everything else, the supreme Pontiffs make this the only business of their life. Here you may see even decrepit old men shewing all the vigour of youth, incurring any expense, deterred by nothing, if only they can overturn law, religion, peace, and throw all the world into confusion." Thirty years later such words would have cost Erasmus dear. For the present the Papacy, secure in its unchallenged power, confident in its strength, bore with easy tolerance the shafts of ridicule which the wandering scholar aimed at it.

His visit to Italy, notwithstanding, was of great importance to Erasmus. It was, as it were, the completion of his twenty years of preparatory study. He was now recognized by the scholars of Italy as their equal and peer. He returned to England in the year 1509, master of all the learning Bologna and Florence and Venice could give him, the intimate friend of the most famous scholars of Italy, strengthened for his future struggle with the monks by influence with the most powerful Cardinals at Rome. As he crossed the Alps on his journey to England, he can scarcely have been ignorant that he, the base-born son of the monk Gerard, himself an apostate monk—for he had lately obtained leave of the Pope to renounce the cowl of his order, was now by universal consent the chief of Transalpine scholars, the supreme Pontiff of the aristocracy of letters. His fame had now spread to every land. Europe was ready to listen with respect to his slightest word.

He was not long in delivering his message, in shewing the direction which the Teutonic Renaissance under his leadership was likely to take. Traveling through Italy and France on his mule, Erasmus had occupied himself with reflections upon what he had seen in Italy and the state of Christendom, which resulted in the production at Sir Thomas More's house of his famous book 'The Praise of Folly.' Ostensibly it is a mere squib, a merry piece of fun, composed by the great scholar to while away days of great suffering by which he was at this time unfitted for serious labor. In reality the 'Praise of Folly' is one of the most powerful satires of a century which produced the 'Epistles of Obscure Men' and More's 'Utopia.' It is a serious indictment of the abuses of the time. Its exposure of the monks and the corruption of the Church did much to prepare the way for the Reformation.

We in this day can scarcely grasp the opportunities possessed by a man of letters who wrote in the common language of the educated of all countries. The 'Encomium Moriæ' ran through seven editions, twenty thousand copies, in a few months. Holbein illustrated it. For years it was constantly being translated or re-edited. A hundred and twenty years later, John Milton found it in everybody's hands at Cambridge. Unlike many of the more scholarly of the works of Erasmus and his contemporaries, which repose decently in undisturbed rest on the shelves of our public libraries, the 'Praise of Folly' still lives, made readable by its blended sense and humour.

The idea of the little book is this. The goddess Folly ascends a rostrum, arrayed in cap and bells, and pronounces upon herself that eulogy which an ungrateful world has forgotten to accord to her. She claims to be the chief of all goddesses, man's best benefactress, the cause of all his happiness, the giver of all his pleasures. "Who knows not," she argues, "that man's childhood is by far the most delightful period of his existence? And why? Because he is then most a fool. And next to that his youth, in which folly still prevails; while in proportion as he retires from her dominion and becomes possessed, through discipline and experience, of mature wisdom, his beauty loses its bloom, his strength declines, his wit becomes less pungent. At last weary old age succeeds, with a weariness which would be absolutely unbearable, did not Folly, in pity of such grievous miseries, give relief by bringing on a second childhood." It is true, she admits,

that Reason also has a share in influencing the life of men, but
then how small a share! Jupiter intended them to be merry, and
took care that reason should exist in due subordination. Moreover, as an antidote to the dangerous effects of wisdom, Folly
herself, had advised the creation of woman—"a foolish, silly
creature, no doubt," she says, "but amusing and agreeable, who
owes to me alone those endowments in which she excels and
surpasses man." Next, we are to mark how dependent we are
upon Folly for the joys of life. She it is who makes friendship
possible by hiding each other's faults. Cupid, too, is a blind little
fool. Woe to society were it otherwise! Self-esteem is only
another form of foolishness, but without it the world could scarce
go on. "Take away this one property of a fool," she argues
wittily, "and the orator shall become as dumb and silent as the
pulpit he stands in; the musician shall hang up his untouched
instrument on the wall; the completest actors shall be hissed off
the stage; the painter shall himself vanish into an imaginary
landscape." On the other hand, what happiness does self-esteem
bring, which so flushes men with a good conceit of their own that
no one repents of his shape, his wit, of his education, or of his
country! so that the dirty half-drowned Hollander would not
remove into the pleasant plains of Italy, nor the brutish Scythian
quit his thorny deserts to become an inhabitant of the Fortunate
Island.

It is a mistake, Folly continues, to pay so much regard to wise
men. Geniuses manage their domestic concerns very badly.
Grave scholars are like death's-heads at a feast, like camels at a
dance, dull and useless in common life, They are no good either
for war or politics. In battle your Demosthenes runs away. The
best soldiers are courageous louts and shallow-brained plow-
boys. As for government and Plato's philosopher-kings, bookish
and learned governors are the worst in the world. A pretty
business the Catos and Gracchi and Brutuses made of it! Even
Antoninus did not do his people so much good by his wisdom as
he did harm by leaving a Commodus to succeed him. Nature,
luckily, takes care that this curse of wisdom shall not become
hereditary. The children of Socrates were dull, insipid souls, or as

some one ingeniously expresses it—" they had more of the mother than the father."

Worst of all, wise men are wretched.   It is the fools who are happy.   Wisdom opens our eyes to the miserable spectacle of the countless ills flesh is heir to: infirmity, disease and death; besides all that man inflicts upon his fellow—a prospect that has to many sages made suicide sweet and welcome.   Were wisdom less rare, all would act thus and the race would become extinct.   The truly happy are the votaries of Folly, on whom shame, disgrace, abuse, fall pointless.   Her blessed illusions are what bind men to life and give them joy.

After more of this admirable fooling, the goddess suddenly forgets herself and becomes serious.   She can joke no longer when she has to speak of schoolmen and theologians, kings and popes and monks, as they were at the end of the fifteenth century.   It is John Colet who speaks now.   Erasmus has at least redeemed his promise to aid him in his crusade both against an obsolete theology and a corrupt and degraded church.   Folly claims the scholastic divines as her peculiar disciples.   "It is by one of my properties, self-love," she says, " that they fancy themselves caught up to the third Heaven, from whence they look down with contempt upon the whole human race as if they were cattle creeping on the ground."   She lashes the commentators, who make darker what was dark before ; the theologians, who explain exactly how the worlds were created and the foundations of the earth were laid—" at whose conjectures," she observes drily, "Nature is mightily amused;" the divines, " who minutely describe everything in the infernal regions as if they had passed many years in that kingdom ; and concludes her attack upon the schoolmen by a modest proposal to send the whole tribe of confident controversialists to do battle against the Turks.   Nothing, she is sure, could stand against their invincible prowess.

The monks fare even worse than the theologians, and Erasmus the Catholic rages against them far more bitterly than any Protestant Foxe or Tyndale.   "These very delightful men," he writes, "who are remarkable for their dirt, their ignorance, their clownish manners, who bellow for bread in front of our doors,

who bray out in church the psalms which they count indeed but
cannot understand, they pretend forsooth that they are the
genuine successors of the Apostles! Their religion consists in
having their dress of the prescribed shape, material, pieces, their
girdle in so many knots, their sleep in so many divisions. They
strive not so much to be like Christ as to be unlike one another.
If they only knew what will befall them on the last day, when the
Judge shall demand to see their works of charity! What will
they have to shew? Bushels of psalms sung, tons of fish eaten;
one will bring his single hood never changed, another the gloves
without which for sixty years he never handled money, others will
point to numbness or paralysis brought on by the confinement of
the cell. But the Judge will interrupt them. 'Whence comes
this new race of Jews! My mansions are promised to deeds of
faith and charity. I will have righteousness and not traditions.'"

We might have expected that Erasmus, a Catholic priest, but
lately at Rome, in favor at the Papal Court, would have spared
Popes and Cardinals. But he does not. He has seen evil and
will denounce it, poor scholar though he is, dependent for his
very bread upon the donations of his friends. "Now as to the
Popes of Rome," he represents his mouth-piece Folly as saying—
"who pretend themselves Christ's vicars, if they would but imitate
His exemplary life in the being attended with poverty, nakedness,
hunger, and a contempt of the world, what order of men would
be in a worse condition? How much of their pleasure would be
abated if they were but endowed with one dram of wisdom? All
their riches, all their honour, their Peter's patrimony, their offices,
their indulgences—in a word, all their perquisites would be
forfeited and lost; and in their room would succeed watchings,
fastings, tears, prayers, hard studies, repenting sighs, and a
thousand such-like severe penalties. The very head of the
Church, the spiritual Prince, would then be brought from all his
splendor to the poor equipage of a scrip and staff. But all this
is upon the supposition only," he concludes with bitter sarcasm,
"that they understood what circumstances they are placed in;
whereas now by a wholesome neglect of thinking, they live as well
as heart can wish: whatever of toil and drudgery belongs to their

office, that they assign over to S. Peter or S. Paul, who have time enough to mind it."

This, then, was the first fruit of the Renaissance working upon the Teutonic mind—simply a moral revolt against the corrupt Christianity of the time. The Humanists of Italy had ceased to believe in the Gospel. The scholars of Germany and England merely appealed from the false Christianity to the true; and it was this moral repulsion from the base and wicked lives of Popes and clergy which made possible the success of Luther. It remains a mystery how they could allow Erasmus to proclaim their shame to the world. Cardinals and worldly Bishops read the 'Praise of Folly' without a protest, with amused indifference, with admiration for this entertaining fellow Erasmus. They did not dream that its destructive criticism might aid in rending the Church asunder. They forgot that all men's consciences were not dead like their own. They forgot that the great heart of the world is just. Pope Leo X. read the book, and merely remarked that Erasmus, too, had his corner in the region of Folly. It was the same Pope, you may remember, who said when he was shewn Martin Luther's ninety-five propositions, "A drunken German wrote them; when he has slept off his wine, he will be of another mind."

Successful as it was and universally read, the 'Praise of Folly' did nothing towards helping Erasmus to live. He never seems to have expected an income from the sale of his books. He wrote because he could not help it, not in order to earn money. And if you ask how he lived, I am afraid one must answer, by constant, pertinacious, shameless begging. Erasmus was the sturdy mendicant of literature, and his letters of this period consist largely of humiliating appeals to his friends for money. He was no longer exactly a poor man. Lord Mountjoy had given him a pension for life of a hundred crowns, Archbishop Warham another of like amount, and every year he received some hundreds of nobles in presents from various patrons scattered all over Europe. He possessed two horses, he himself tells us, "better fed than their owner, and a couple of grooms better clothed than their master." His friends, Colet and Linacre, from time to time seem to have given him the hint to live more economically, and in modern times, harsh critics of his career, like Mr. Froude, have accused him of being a lover of pleasure, " a clever, healthy, epicurean man of the world." Nothing could be more scandalously unjust. Erasmus was really a devoted, hard-working scholar, whose profession necessitated constant journeys to consult books and manuscripts, whose frail health and diseased body made poverty doubly hard. It is pitiable, no doubt, to read the letters in which he begs for money, presses Colet for a few crowns, and blames Linacre for his stinginess, but the shame of it does not belong entirely to Erasmus. Here was a man, doing work for Europe that no other scholar in the world could do, living centuries before the time when an author could expect from an impersonal public an honourable reward, in an epoch which saw a Wolsey rise from obscurity to boundless wealth, at a time when abject flattery and ignoble services could earn bishoprics and cardinals' hats: bravely refusing to cringe and flatter, denouncing, as courageous men of letters have done in every age, the crimes of the great and powerful, compelled to sue to friends for a modest sustenance. I say the shame is not his. We do not love Dean Colet when he writes to Erasmus, " If you beg humbly I have something for you ; but if you ask immodestly, poverty must help poverty, to say the least, very poorly. You will do well in my opinion to imitate Diogenes." We admire, rather, the ever generous and sympathetic Archbishop Warham. " I send you thirty angels," he writes. " I wish there were ten legions of them. Use them for the recovery of your health, and I only wish I could purchase health for you for a much larger sum. Take good care of yourself, and do not defraud me by your illness of the brilliant hopes I have entertained of you, and of the fruit of your learning."

Erasmus had returned to England in the hope of obtaining that independence which he felt was not to be had under Papal patronage at Rome ; and in 1511, this hope seemed about to be realized, when, by the influence of Fisher, Bishop of Rochester, one of the best friends of the New Learning, he was appointed Lady Margaret Professor of Divinity and in some sort reader in Greek at Cambridge. Cambridge, however, was not kind to Erasmus.

His enemies, the scholastic divines, still flourished there, and the University was a little behind the times, being scarcely as far advanced as Oxford was when Erasmus first visited it fourteen years before. His lectures on the Greek language were badly attended, and at the end of two years, having almost completed the great work of his life—his edition and translation of the New Testament, he was thoroughly discontented, and ready to set out on his travels again. "I have been living for some months," he writes in 1513 to his friend Ammonius, "the life of a snail, shut up at home and buried in my books. Cambridge is a complete desert; most of the men are away for fear of the plague, though when they are all here, even then it is a desert. The expense is intolerable, and there is not a farthing to get. I am determined now to leave no stone unturned, and, as they say, to cast my sheet anchor. If I succeed, I shall make my nest. If not, I shall flit."

There is one episode of his stay at Cambridge which I ought to notice before I pass on, because it illustrates exactly the attitude of the Oxford Reformers to the ecclesiastical questions of the time, and the direction which they thought reform should take. In one of his best-known books, his 'Colloquies,' Erasmus has given us an account of a pilgrimage which about this time John Colet and himself made to the famous shrine of Thomas à Becket at Canterbury. They were shewn the dagger of the saint, his skull cased in silver, and a perfect mine of bones; all of which they were expected to kiss, much to Colet's disgust. He seems to have behaved indeed as badly as any Protestant could have done. When the shrine of S. Thomas was displayed, blazing in gold and jewels, he enquired from the guide whether S. Thomas when he was alive was not very kind to the poor. The verger assented. "Then," said Colet, "he would probably prefer that these vast riches should go to lighten the burden of poor men's poverty rather than that they should be hoarded here, useless to any one." This, however, was not the worst. By and bye, the prior of Canterbury, knowing Colet's distinguished position, opened a chest, and taking out several dilapidated rags which S. Thomas was reputed to have used to wipe his brow, offered one of them to Colet as a present of untold value. "Again," says

Erasmus, "my friend was very rude. He touched the rag with the tips of his fingers, with a look of great disgust, and contemptuously put it down, making at the same time a sort of whistle, as was his way when displeased. I was ashamed of him, but the Prior wisely took no notice of his rudeness, and shortly took his leave. On our departure from Canterbury we passed through a lane where a mendicant monk sprinkled us with holy water and invited Colet to kiss a shoe, which he said was a relic of S. Thomas. "What!" Colet said to me passionately, "do these idiots expect us to kiss the shoe of every good man?" So ended this curious pilgrimage of these precursors of the Reformation. "In that meeting," says Dean Stanley, "of the old monk with the two strangers in the Canterbury lane, how completely do we read, in miniature, the whole history of the coming revolution in Europe."

The year 1514 found Erasmus at Basle, which henceforth, though he continued his restless wanderings, became his head-quarters and his real home. Here he formed a close friend-ship with the great printer Froben, one of those scholarly men without whose enthusiastic help the Revival of Learning must have been long delayed, from whose press at this time new editions of Greek and Roman classics, of the writings of the Fathers, of the New Testament itself, began to issue every year.

We may regard the period which we have now reached, that which elapses between the year 1514 and the outbreak of the Reformation struggle, as the happiest and most prosperous, the most useful and fertile in great works, of the whole life of Erasmus. He was now beyond the reach of poverty. Offers of promotion and honourable posts reached him from every court in Europe: from the Emperor Charles V., from the King of France, from Pope Adrian VI. Amongst men of letters north of the Alps, he was without a rival. His works were universally read; he had carried the educated world with him; his enemies were discredited; scholasticism was dying; the New Learning was everywhere triumphing. "Had Erasmus departed from the world at this time," says Dean Milman, "it might have been

happier perhaps for himself—happier, no doubt, for his fame.
His character, in spite of infirmities, would have been well-nigh
blameless. Though not himself, strictly speaking, to have been
enrolled in the noble and martyr band of the assertors of religious
freedom, he would have been honoured as the most illustrious of
their precursors and prophets, as having done more than any one
to break the bonds of scholasticism, superstition, ignorance, and
sacerdotal tyranny."

Of the books of this period, many in number, most of them
memorable, there are two only which I have time to notice. The
first of these is the 'Novum Instrumentum,' as Erasmus called it,
his edition of the Greek text of the New Testament, accompanied
by a fresh Latin translation of his own. It is a work which every
one ought to know something about. "It contributed more,"
says Mr. Mark Pattison, "to the liberation of the human mind
from the thraldom of the mediæval clergy than all the uproar and
rage of Luther's many pamphlets." What then exactly, was it, we
may ask, that Erasmus effected? The answer must be, that through
his agency the world was placed in possession of printed copies of
the New Testament, not in a Latin translation, but in the original
Greek. For centuries the Church had used no other version but
the Vulgate, the Latin translation due mainly to S. Jerome, which
alone was quoted by divines, and every word of which was regarded
by them as supernaturally inspired. It required the utmost daring
in the beginning of the sixteenth century even to hint that the
Vulgate was not always accurate. It seems incredible, but men
had largely forgotten that S. Paul and S. John did not write in
Latin, and the outcry was great when Erasmus printed the original
Greek text. He was correcting the Holy Ghost, the theologians
said. "It cannot be," wrote one, "that the unanimous universal
Church now for so many centuries has been mistaken, which has
always used the Vulgate version. Many will doubt if they learn
that even one jot or tittle in the Holy Scriptures is false; and then
will come to pass what Augustine described to Jerome, 'If any
error should be admitted to have crept into the Holy Scriptures,
what authority would be left to them?'" Erasmus, however, was
not deterred, and held on his way undismayed. He was confident

of the truth of Christianity, and was the strongest opponent of the
sceptical scholars of Italy; but he would not blind his eyes to
manifest facts. He was as fervent a believer in the Bible as
Martin Luther himself, and in his preface to his New Testament
there is a noble passage which William Tyndale might have
written. "I altogether and utterly dissent," he says, "from those
who are unwilling that the Holy Scriptures, translated into the
vulgar tongue, should be read by private persons, as though the
teachings of Christ were so abstruse as to be intelligible only to a
few theologians, or as though the safety of Scripture rested on
man's ignorance of it. It may be well to conceal the mysteries of
kings; but Christ willed that His mysteries should be published as
widely as possible. I wish that even the weakest woman should
read the Gospel—should read the Epistles of St. Paul. I long
that the husbandman should sing portions of them to himself as
he follows the plough, that the weaver should hum them to the
tune of his shuttle, that the traveler should beguile with their
stories the tedium of his journey."—Notwithstanding, he will not
consent to stultify his reason, and in the best sense of the word he
was a rationalist critic of the Bible. He fearlessly cast out from
his edition spurious texts like that of the 'three Heavenly Witnesses' which remained in our English Bibles until the other day.
Following his great master, S. Jerome, he denied verbal inspira-
tion, and pointed out that when S. Mark wrote Abiathar, he made
a mistake for Ahimelech, and that often when the Apostles quote
from the Old Testament they do not give the exact words of the
original. He had doubts as to whether S. John wrote the Apo-
calypse, and felt convinced that the Epistle to the Hebrews was
not written by S. Paul. He blundered often enough, it is true, as
was inevitable to a pioneer in a new path, but in a very real and
true sense he is entitled to be called the father of modern Biblical
criticism.

. It was not, however, views of this kind which gave the greatest
offence to the monks and theologians. It was bad enough that a
man should presume to correct the sacred Vulgate, and to remind
divines that they were ignorant of the language in which the
original documents of Christianity were written, but in his notes

and annotations to his New Testament, Erasmus assailed the popular religion of his day in the most uncompromising manner, and
struck at every abuse of the Church as boldly as Wycliffe or
Luther.   He attacked auricular confession, fasts and feasts, relics
and pilgrimages, even the celibacy of the clergy.   He denied that
the words, "Upon this rock I will build my church," applied
exclusively to the Pope.   He refers contemptuously to the " mira-
culous oil exhibited in the churches, the fragments of the Cross in
such quantities that if they could be brought together it would take
a merchant vessel to hold them all."   In his note on S. Paul's
statement that he preached the Gospel without charge, he says,
"That was a boast truly worthy of an Apostle, but one which no
one in our days is ambitious of making.   Nothing is to be had
now without money.   You cannot even get buried free of cost."

Six years later he continued and developed these teachings in
the most famous of all his works, the 'Colloquies,' which was
published in 1522.   It is a collection of dialogues and satires, free
and outspoken as ever—in spite of the fact that Luther had been
condemned by the Pope and the Reformation struggle had begun
—against the corruptions of Christianity.   No book of his is more
characteristic of Erasmus than this; in its humour, its common
sense, its detestation of falsehood and tyranny, its fervent appeals
on behalf of high and noble living.   His tolerance is shown when
he declines to consign to damnation the good men of antiquity,
and wishes that more Christians could die like Socrates.   He
comes very closely to the modern spirit when he asks: May not
matrimony be as pure as celibacy?   Can we not trust that the
God of love will be as open to our prayers as any of His saints?
What undutiful duteousness it is to go on pilgrimage to Jerusa-
lem and leave a wife and little children uncared-for at home?   Is
it not absurd to see the treasures of saints who, when on earth,
gave all to the poor?   Is not baptism a sufficient renunciation of
the world, without taking monastic vows as well?   How many,
like the Pharisees, stop at ceremonies and never aim at charity?
Do the begging friars remember the words, "It is more blessed to
give than to receive," or the ascetics that the Son of Man came
eating and drinking?

Once more, we have to ask in vain: How did Erasmus escape being punished as a heretic? It was not until 1526 that the University of Paris condemned the 'Colloquies' as a work in which the author, " like a heathen, ridicules, satirizes, and sneers at the Christian religion and its holy ceremonies and observances." It was not until after his death that the Inquisition placed the book upon the Index, and forbade any loyal Catholic to read it.

We come now to the most important and difficult problem in the life of Erasmus, his attitude toward Luther and the Reformation. How is it, we hear it continually asked, that this man who hated monkery, ridiculed relics and pilgrimages and prayers to the saints, disbelieved in confession and celibacy, venerated the Scripture, and declined to allow complete autocracy to the Papacy, who longed to cleanse the Church of its corruptions and restore Christianity to its primitive purity—how is it that he, like Sir Thomas More, his fellow-disciple, is found at last in hostility to Luther, on the side of Romanism and the Pope?

The popular theory seems to be that Erasmus would have sided with Luther if he had not been a coward, too fond of his ease and his reputation to battle for a cause which he knew in his heart to be just: that he, in fact, sacrificed his convictions to his interests, and sold himself to the devil. "He knew Luther to be right," says Froude, in his brilliant and most misleading essay on the subject. " Luther had but said what Erasmus all his life had been convinced of, and Luther looked to see him come forward and take his place at his side. Had Erasmus done so, the course of events would have been far happier and better. But there would have been some danger—danger to the leaders, if certainty of triumph to the cause—and Erasmus had no gift of martyrdom."

No gift of martyrdom! It is true. Erasmus, it may be freely admitted, had not the moral heroism of Luther. It is difficult to imagine him confronting an assembly of eager enemies thirsting for his death, and boldly throwing down his gage of battle: " Here stand I. I will not retract. God help me. Amen." No doubt the chief fault of Erasmus was timidity, the timidity of a toil-worn scholar, growing old, longing for peace, made weak by fifty years' struggle against the most painful and distracting

malady known to man. "Not every one has strength for martyrdom," he himself wrote, with noble humility: "If I were put in
S. Peter's place, I fear I should imitate S. Peter."

The truth, however, seems to be this. Erasmus has been
traduced by both Catholics and Protestants. His influence
was the most important and weighty in all Europe, and both
parties strove hard to win him for their own. But he belonged
to neither of them. He occupied a middle position, too much a
Reformer for monks and Papal theologians, too little a revolutionist for Luther and his followers. He was the Lord Falkland
of the Reformation, and, like Lord Falkland, he has been accused
of cowardice and inconsistency, irresolution and treason to the
right, when his real crime was that he was too clear-sighted to
become a narrow partisan, too honest to shut his eyes to the
grievous faults on both sides. All honour to martyrs: to Luther
with his single-hearted devotedness to what he believed to be the
truth, to Sir Thomas More with his noble sacrifice of his life in a
cause he believed to be sacred! But whose heart does not go out
in sympathy to this maligned scholar, who had spent his existence
in brave battling against corruption and wickedness, now made the
mark for violent abuse and coarse invective, condemned by all later
generations as a coward and a time-server because he was too con-
scientious to join heartily with Pope and Cardinals against Luther,
too far-sighted to welcome with delight the prospect of a divided
Christendom and centuries of horrible civil war waged in the name
of religion, which he saw Luther's violent policy would make
inevitable? It is idle to complain that he did not take his stand
by Luther's side, that he was not ready to die in defence of Luther's
doctrines. He had no belief in them. Mr. Froude is positively
mistaken when he declares that Erasmus knew Luther to be in
the right. The two men agreed only in denouncing the abuses of
Catholicism, the worship of relics, the corruption of the monastic
orders, the worldly and evil lives of Bishops and Cardinals, and so
forth; otherwise they were as far asunder as the poles. For Luther's
dogma of justification by faith, rightly or wrongly, Erasmus
had the greatest abhorrence. He hated theological metaphysics,
and his common sense revolted against Luther's strenuous assertion

of the non-freedom of the human will, which lay at the root of all his teaching. Erasmus treated it as an absurd paradox. Luther says of it, "This matter is to me serious, necessary, and eternal, more momentous than life itself, and to be asserted, even should it plunge the world into conflict, or bring it to chaos." He did not shrink from the most extreme inferences that could be drawn from his favourite doctrine, and when Erasmus inquired what men would take trouble to amend their lives if they had satisfied themselves that all their actions were pre-determined and necessary, he boldly replied; "No one will amend his life; the elect will have theirs amended for them; the non-elect must perish in their misery." That fatal sentence of his is almost sufficient justification of the position of Erasmus, from which he never swerved: "Do the will of Christ, and leave dark mysteries alone."

It is difficult again to see why he should be blamed for not following the example of Luther in rebelling against the Papacy and dividing the Christian Church. Luther, at the beginning of his reforming career, believed in the Papacy as much as he did. He did not turn against the Pope until the Pope turned against him, and we have his own word for it that if Leo X. had given way on two points—the granting of the cup to the laity and marriage to the clergy—there would have been no schism. The difference between the two men lay here. Both aimed at reforms in the Catholic Church. Erasmus believed that they could be brought about gradually, peacefully, by the spread of education, without destroying the unity of the Church and plunging Europe into centuries of fratricidal war. Luther, on the contrary, was a violent revolutionist, prepared to break with the past, ready to sacrifice unity and brotherhood for what he believed to be the victory of truth. I do not contend that Luther was wrong and Erasmus right. Certainly, we have paid a heavy price for the freedom which the Reformation gave; but it may have been inevitable. It may well have been that the Church was too corrupt to be cleansed by the moderate and peaceful methods of the Oxford Reformers. The dream of Erasmus of a broad, comprehensive, tolerant Catholic Church, whose enforced dogmas should be few, whose theology should be simple, whose prelates should be servants of the people, whose dignitaries should imitate the poverty, humility, the self-sacrifice of Christ, whose ministers should be the first to raise their voices on behalf of the poor and oppressed, whose aim should be to put an end to war and tyranny and needless suffering and to inaugurate the Kingdom of God upon earth—this no doubt was too noble an ideal for the sixteenth century to attain to, nor has the nineteenth realized it. But for all that, the life of Erasmus, though it went out in pain and anguish and gloom, amid the crash and storm of the Reformation conflict, was not a failure. The world would not listen to him then. It is listening now.

LECTURE III.

Sir Thomas More.

"*It is unfortunate for More's reputation that he has been adopted as the champion of a party and a cause which is arrayed in hostility to the liberties and constitution of his country. Apart from the partisan use which is made of his name, we must rank him amongst the noblest minds of England, as one who became the victim of a tyrant whose policy he disapproved and whose servile instruments he despised.*"—MARK PATTISON.

"*Of all men nearly perfect, Sir Thomas More had, perhaps, the clearest marks of individual character. His peculiarities, though distinguishing him from all others, were yet withheld from growing into moral faults. It is not enough to say of him that he was unaffected, that he was natural, that he was simple; so the larger part of truly great men have been. But there is something homespun in More which is common to him with scarcely any other. This quality bound together his genius and learning, his eloquence and fame, with his homely and daily duties, bestowing a genuineness on all his good qualities, a dignity on the most ordinary offices of life, and an accessible familiarity on the virtues of a hero and a martyr, which silences every suspicion that his excellences were magnified.*"—SIR JAMES MACKINTOSH.

"*One of the marvels of More was his infinite variety. He could write epigrams in a hair shirt at the Carthusian Convent; and pass from translating Lucian to lecturing on Augustine at the Church of S. Lawrence. Devout almost to superstition, he was lighthearted almost to buffoonery. One hour we see him encouraging Erasmus in his love of Greek and the New Learning, or charming with his ready wit the supper-tables of the Court, or turning a debate in Parliament; the next at home, surrounded by friends and familiar servants, by wife and children, and children's children, dwelling among them in an atmosphere of love and music, prayers and irony—throwing the rein, as it were, on the neck of his most careless fancies, and condescending to follow out the humours of his monkey and the fool. His fortune was almost as various. From his utter indifference to show and money, he must have been a strange successor to Wolsey. He had thought as little about fame as Shakspere; yet in the next generation it was an honour to an Englishman throughout Europe to be the countryman of More.*"—Edinburgh Review, 1846.

LECTURE III.

THOMAS MORE was born, it is now clearly established, in the year 1478, seven years after Machiavelli, five years before Luther. We shall perhaps be better able to understand him if we remember that two years before his birth William Caxton set up the first English printing press at Westminster, and that when he was a lad of fourteen Christopher Columbus set forth on his first voyage of discovery. More's father was a prosperous barrister, who afterwards became Sir John More, and a judge in the Court of King's Bench. He sent his son, after the custom of the time, to be brought up in the household of one of the great men of the day, Cardinal Morton, Archbishop of Canterbury, and prime minister to that royal miser, Henry VII. The Cardinal lives in some of our older histories as a financier and an extortioner, and especially as the witty inventor of 'Morton's fork.' It was part of his business to fleece as extensively as possible the merchants of London in order to swell the King's treasury. When they appeared before him to settle the amount of their taxes or loans, he would tell those who came richly attired, that as they were evidently wealthy they could afford to give largely; while on the other hand, those who came meanly and poorly dressed, he accused of saving money, and made them pay handsomely also. Morton, however, deserves to be remembered as a generous benefactor of learning, and above all as having been the first to detect the extraordinary talents of young More. "Whosoever shall live to see it," he used to tell his guests, "this child waiting at table shall prove a rare and notable man." It was one of the pleasures of rich noblemen and prelates of that age, who recognised that wealth has its duties as well as its rights, to give to youths of great abilities and slender means, the opportunity of becoming learned men. It was the generous support extended to him when poor by an English nobleman, Lord Mountjoy, which enabled Erasmus to become the leading scholar in Europe. Similarly, More was sent to Oxford at Cardinal Morton's expense,

He found the University in the ferment of an intellectual revolution, caused by the teachings of scholars like Grocyn and Colet, who were opening to eager students the treasures of Greek literature. As a consequence new doctrines in science, in politics, in religion, began to be preached, and the older teachers grew alarmed. They detested the new studies and charged the Greek students with heresy and infidelity. Like many foolish persons since, they appealed to the wisdom of their ancestors: what was good enough for their fathers was good enough for them. More ranged himself at once on the side of the New Learning, and became Colet's loyal and enthusiastic disciple.

He was not allowed, however, to stay long at Oxford. His father, an orthodox person of the old school, anxious above all things for his son to become a successful barrister, took fright when he heard of the new-fangled dangerous Greek studies, and removed him to the law schools in London. Here More devoted himself to his profession, and rapidly came to the front. But he did not forget Erasmus and Colet, nor the New Learning, and so we find him at the age of twenty-three, lecturing on S. Augustine's 'City of God' to an audience which included all the learned men of the time.

The year 1504 saw him in Parliament, and at once an opportunity was given of shewing what was the attitude of men of the New Learning to politics. That was the age, as every one knows, of slavish and subservient Parliaments, and this was the most subservient of all, controlled by the two ministers of Henry's avarice, Empson and Dudley. In 1504 the King was about to marry his eldest daughter to the Scottish King, and was legally entitled to demand from Parliament a grant of about £30,000. Instead of that, however, his ministers asked for a subsidy of £113,000; and the House of Commons, afraid to resist the extortion, was about to pass the grant, when Thomas More, the youngest burgess in the House, rose in his place and delivered so eloquent and energetic a protest, that when it came to a decision the King's demand was cut down to one-fourth of what he had asked. More's conduct was reported to the King by his officials, who informed him that all his plans had been defeated by a "beardless boy."

Those were not days when it was altogether safe to oppose the wishes of the sovereign, or to take a patriotic course in Parliament, and the ignoble King soon found means of punishment. He threw More's father into prison and compelled him to pay a fine, while More himself was obliged to retire from public life, and at one time seriously contemplated leaving the country.

In his retirement, there came upon him again a longing, which had never left him, to follow the example of the saintliest Christians of the last five centuries and enter a monastery. There had always been two tendencies struggling for mastery within him— one the monkish, ascetic ideal of the Middle Ages—the other, the ideal of a freer, wider Christianity formulated by the men of the New Learning. At one time, accordingly, we find him deep in classical studies, writing stinging epigrams against tyranny, and perfecting himself in music, his passionate delight; while shortly afterwards, it is recorded of him that he took lodgings near the Charterhouse, and subjected himself daily to the most painful austerities of the most severe of monks. It seemed exceedingly probable in the year 1505 that More would take upon himself religious vows and end his days in a monastery. He was saved from such a career, partly by the influence of his humanist friends, partly by finding that the religious orders were corrupt, and that the cloister was not the most favorable place in the world just then for a pious and useful life.

When we next catch a glimpse of More, he is married, in full practice at the bar, with all monastic dreams thrown to the winds. His marriage deserves a word of notice. Those were the days of unromantic unions, and More's was no exception, but there is a touch of Quixotic chivalry about it which makes it interesting. The wife he chose was Jane Colt, the daughter of an Essex gentleman. Let me quote to you the account of the matter given by William Roper, his son-in-law, whose quaint simple, biography contains most of what we know concerning More. "Although," says Roper, "Master More's mind most served him to the second daughter of Mr. Colt, for that he thought her the fairest and best favoured; yet when he considered that it would be both great grief and some shame also to the eldest to see her younger sister in marriage preferred before her, he then of a certain pity framed his fancy towards her and soon after married her." I presume that, in spite of the lamentable lack of romance in this episode, there is a height of heroic virtue in it of which most of us do not feel ourselves capable. The marriage, however, proved an ideal one. More devoted himself tenderly to the young girl whom he had thus chosen, teaching her music and languages, making her the associate of his intellectual life; and when, unhappily, she died in early youth, he transferred his affection to their eldest daughter Margaret, destined thereafter to become one of the most celebrated women in Europe.

His second marriage was entered into purely for the sake of his little children, and it would seem that, like Socrates before him, Richard Hooker and many another great man after him, More was unfortunate. Dame Alice Middleton, his second wife, appears from all descriptions to have been an exceedingly commonplace, stupid and worldly woman, in every way the exact opposite of her husband and admirably calculated to drive him to distraction and despair. More's sunny good nature, however, conquered every obstacle. No word of complaint ever escaped him. She was, he admits, "nec bella nec puella," but says Erasmus, "More lived with her on such terms of respect and kindness as if she had been both." William Roper tells us that he lived in the same house with More for sixteen years, and never once saw him in a temper, or heard him use a harsh or ungentle word. His home life, indeed, constitutes an ideal which has never been surpassed.

When Henry VII. died, all obstacles to More's success in life vanished, and his rise in his profession became unprecedentedly rapid. He was engaged in every important case in the courts, earned an income of about £5,000 of our money, attracted the attention of the young King by winning a lawsuit for the Pope against him, was knighted and made a Privy Councillor, and constantly employed on embassies to the continent. These successes, however, were common to him with others. What was peculiar to More was his view of the legal profession, which I am afraid even at this day would be denounced as Utopian and impossible. Nevertheless it remains true that in that far-off, barbarian century, the leading barrister in England laid down these three rules of conduct and kept them. Firstly, when people came to him eager to go to law with their adversaries, he invariably tried to induce them to settle their quarrels without an appeal to the law courts. One shudders to think of the fate of any unhappy lawyer of to-day who should venture upon conduct so entirely unprofessional. Secondly, he had so absurd and fantastic a notion of rectitude, that he would never undertake a cause of whose justice he was not beforehand thoroughly convinced. And, thirdly, he would never receive a farthing in fees from widows or orphans or poor people. There is enough, surely, in such conduct of a barrister to entitle him to the name of a social reformer, even if he had never written the 'Utopia.'

And now let me turn to that most remarkable book of his, the first product of Renaissance free thought in the English language. The 'Utopia' is a work which in our busy century, distracted as it is by an immense variety of intellectual interests, every one knows about and few people read. I respectfully submit to you that the ideas of a renowned scholar, of the most famous English man of letters of his generation, upon some of the most important questions of human life, are worth perusal, even though they are nearly four centuries old. And for these reasons. Whatever other value the 'Utopia' may have, it is absolutely indispensable to the historical student as a revelation of the social condition of our country in early Tudor times. Next it is important as being the first fruits in English literature of that great revival of learning, of that new birth of knowledge, which makes the early sixteenth century the seed-time of modern civilization, You can trace in it also the marks of the wide difference which separates the Revival of Learning in Italy from the corresponding movement in our

own country. More was not the only scholar who put forth
to the world at this period a treatise on government and the
well-being of States. At the very time when he was preparing
the 'Utopia,' another great thinker, Machiavelli of Florence, was
composing that little book, 'The Prince,' which became the hand-
book of kings and statesmen for a century. The contrast
between these two is instructive. One discovers that whereas in
Italy the revolt against the Middle Ages and the Revival of
Learning meant Paganism in religion, utter degradation in morals,
tyranny, craft and selfishness in statesmanship; in England,
through the influence of men like Erasmus and Colet and More,
the Renaissance was Christian in its tendencies, filled with visions
of a higher and nobler morality, fervently devoted to the cause of
liberty and good government, and maintaining above all things
that the sovereign exists for the people, not the people for the
sovereign. Free thought in Italy produced only great learning
and great license : in England it took a religious form. Free
thought in Italy, fed though it was on the best models of Greece
and Rome, allied itself with tyranny and led to the Age of the
Despots. Free thought in England produced not only the protest
of More, but also the great rebellion of the seventeenth century
against Stuart despotism. Furthermore, the 'Utopia' must take its
place in literature amongst those speculative productions of the
human mind of which Plato's 'Republic' is the first and greatest
example. Practical Englishmen, to whom for the most part
Providence has denied the gift of imagination, are inclined to
regard such works with some degree of impatience and scorn. A
great and honoured Englishman, for example, Mr. John Bright,
told us some years ago, without any apparent bashfulness or
shame, that the best part of Professor Jowett's translation of
Plato's 'Republic' was the translator's excellent English, Plato's
subject matter being considered almost worthless. However, in
More's 'Utopia' there is comfort for us. He was a shrewd, hard-
headed Englishman himself, and this work of his is differentiated
entirely from all other ideal commonwealths by this—that it is
not merely a picture of perfection, nor a speculation as to what
might be if men were angels, but it also contains a practical

programme of reform in English society which, to a large extent, has been realized. Without doubt that is the peculiar interest of the 'Utopia,' that for two centuries we have been slowly, surely, approaching More's ideal and converting his dreams into accomplished facts. Let me take one or two instances out of many. We pride ourselves to-day—do we not?—a good deal on our enlightened measures to prevent increase of crime by good government and education. That idea is first found in More's 'Utopia.' He denounces the system of pure repression and brutal punishment. "If," he says, "you suffer your people to be ill educated, and their manners to be corrupted from their infancy, and then punish them for those crimes to which their first education disposed them, what else is to be concluded from this, but that you first make thieves and then punish them ? "

Again, it has been one of the great social reformations of the nineteenth century that through the efforts of Sir Samuel Romilly, Sir James Mackintosh, and their co-workers, the barbarous criminal code, which punished nearly two hundred offences with death, has been abolished. It was not Sir Samuel Romilly, however, but Sir Thomas More, three centuries ahead of his time, who first urged with passionate earnestness the plea that no man should be put to death for theft and other venial offences. "If, by the Mosaical law," argued More, "though it was rough and severe as being laid upon a people obstinate and servile, men were only fined and not put to death for theft, we cannot imagine that in the new law of mercy, God has given us a greater license to cruelty than He did to the Jews. It is plain and obvious, that it is absurd and of ill consequence to the commonwealth, that a thief and a murderer should be equally punished. Extreme justice is extreme injury."

Again, if there is one blessing more than another which we prize in this age, it is the privilege of every man to hold what religious belief seems best to himself, without persecution, without let or hindrance from any one. I do not say that the old bad spirit of persecution for religious opinions is entirely extinct, but at any rate it is ashamed of itself, and the power of imposing penalties upon one's neighbour for his differences of religious creed is

rapidly disappearing. Now the very idea of toleration in religion,
that great, prominent feature of modern life, was first given to
England by Sir Thomas More. He is as much the original discoverer of it as Columbus was of the islands of America, or Sir
Isaac Newton of the doctrine of gravitation. "The founder of
Utopia," he tells us, "made a law that every man might be of
what religion he pleased, and might endeavour to draw others to
it by the force of argument and by amicable and modest ways, but
without bitterness against those of other opinions." The history
of toleration is but a commentary on those words of More's, and
it may be doubted whether we have yet sufficiently honoured the
noble genius and nobler heart of the man who, three hundred and
seventy years ago, with the mental mists and darkness of the
Middle Ages still about him, gave utterance to such a thought.

Whatever faults it may have as a literary composition, the
'Utopia' is not deficient in humour. Like all the work both of
Erasmus and More, it abounds in delicate irony, and quiet,
sometimes almost imperceptible, satirical touches. No one who
will read between the lines, and who knows anything of the history
of the time, can possibly find it dull. Here are one or two instances
taken at random. One of the chief evils of More's life was the
number and corruption of the monks. "In Utopia," he writes
gravely, "all the priests are men of eminent piety; therefore, their
number is few." There was a foolish rage in England in Henry's
reign for jewels and precious stones for use in dress. "In Utopia,"
says More contemptuously, "they find pearls on their coast, diamonds and carbuncles on their rocks; with these they adorn their
children, who are delighted with them and glory in them during
their childhood; but when they grow to years and see that none
but children use such baubles, they, of their own accord, lay them
aside, and would be as much ashamed to use them afterwards, as
children among us, when they come to years, are of their puppets
and other toys." Gold and silver, too, were despised in Utopia
as metals of little use, and, very significantly, were used to make
fetters for slaves. Apparently, More had a poor opinion of the
English field sports of his time, for he remarks that "among the
Utopians all this business of hunting is turned over to their

butchers: and they look upon hunting as one of the basest parts
of a butcher's work.''

Occasionally, More's satire is delightfully delicate, as when he
tells us that in his imaginary State, no leagues, or treaties, or
alliances are ever made with other nations, the Utopians having
no belief in them. He then observes with a quiet chuckle,
"Perhaps they would change their mind if they lived amongst
us." He lived in an age of abominable and lying diplomacy,
when neither King, nor Emperor, nor Pope could be trusted to
keep his word a day longer than it profited him. This is More's
way of striking a blow at the prevailing Machiavellianism of the
time. "We know," he says ironically, "how religiously treaties are
observed in Europe, more particularly where the Christian doctrine
is received, which is partly owing to the justice and goodness of the
princes themselves, and partly to the reverence they pay to the
Popes, who, as they are most religious observers of their own
promises, so they exhort all other princes to perform theirs "—all
of which was, as we know, the exact contrary of the actual
fact.

There is, unfortunately, no book yet printed which deals thoroughly with the difficulties of the 'Utopia,' and possibly it may be
useful, for those who intend to read it for themselves, to give one
or two hints as to its interpretation. In the first place, then, we
must remember that the glaring absurdities and occasional puer-
ilities which it contains are purposely thrown in to give it the air
of a romance, and to conceal its serious aims. Secondly, irony
and satire predominate throughout, and sometimes More attributes
to the Utopians bad and immoral customs actually prevailing in
Europe. Dull readers say, how shocking! But More's latent
argument is: these things are bad in these benighted pagans of
Utopia; how much more to be condemned, then, amongst the
Christians of Europe! Thirdly, the one deadly heresy about the
'Utopia,' the one absolute misunderstanding of it, is this: to
believe that More was not in earnest—that his book has no real,
serious meaning. We may recall, in this particular, some weighty
words of Ruskin. "The entire purpose of a great thinker," he
warns us in one of his books, "may be difficult to fathom, and we

may be over and over again more or less mistaken in guessing at his meaning; but the real, profound, nay, quite bottomless and unredeemable mistake, is the fool's thought: that he had no meaning."

It would be impossible to describe accurately the institutions of More's ideal State in fewer words than he has used himself, but roughly the main ideas of the Utopian Commonwealth are these. It is based on Communism,—not the Communism of Plato, but of the early Christian Church.   Dean Hook held the strange and impossible view that the 'Utopia' was meant to be a satire against Communism; but there cannot be the least doubt that, in the abstract, as an ideal, More believed in Communism, and looked back longingly to the golden age of Christianity, when not one of the believers "said that aught of the things which he possessed was his own, but they had all things common."   Communism in our time has a bad name, but it was realized constantly on a small scale in the monasteries of the Middle Ages, and flourishes to-day in several societies of the United States. There are even some amongst our great scholars and thinkers of the present age who, like the Fathers, Ambrose and Chrysostom, believe that the dream of Christian Communism will yet be converted into deed.   "When modern individualism," says Renan, "has borne its last fruits; when humanity, dwarfed, dismal, shall return to great institutions and their strong discipline: when our paltry, shopkeeping society—I say rather when our world of pigmies—shall have been driven out with scourges by the heroic and idealistic portions of humanity, then life in common will be realized again."

The objection, of course, the valid objection to Communism, is that it pre-supposes the death of human selfishness. More saw this clearly, and warns us that Communism is an institution of an ideal society.   "There are many things in the Commonwealth of Utopia, that I rather wish than hope to see followed in our governments.   All things will not be well till all men are good, which will not be these many years."   Nevertheless, he does not scruple to declare as an abstract doctrine, in the words of his traveler Raphael, "I am persuaded, that till property is taken away, there can be no equitable or just distribution of things, nor can the world be happily governed ; for as long as that is maintained, the greatest and the far best part of mankind will be still oppressed with a load of cares and anxieties. I confess, without taking it quite away, those pressures that lie on a great part of mankind may be made lighter ; but they can never be quite removed." Decidedly, I am afraid, whether we like it or not, we must believe that Sir Thomas More, in his abstract opinions, as also in his daily life, had strong leanings towards Communism.

The leading principle in the ' Utopia ' may be taken to be this. *It is a commonwealth in which the interests of the whole people are considered to be the first and only rule of the State.* There are no leisured classes. All persons, even the magistrates themselves, and not omitting the women, labour with their hands. But the day's work is limited, not as Mr. Green has it in his History, to nine hours a day, but to six. It is objected to More that six hours labour per day would not produce sufficient to support the needs of humanity. It would be ample, he replied, if first of all, men would limit themselves to necessaries of existence and give up useless luxuries, and secondly, if there were no lazy people living on the labour of others. He then enumerates a list of the idle classes, which must be painful reading to some of us. "First," he says, " women generally do little, who are the half of mankind ; and if some few women are diligent, their husbands are idle. Then consider the great company of idle priests, and of those that are called religious men ; add to those, all rich men, chiefly those that have estates in land, who are called noblemen and gentlemen, together with their families, *i. e.,* servants, made up of idle persons, that are kept more for show than use."

In very many ways, apart from Communistic dreams, one is obliged to admit the ' Utopia ' presents an attractive picture, very largely because in so many matters it embodies the ideals which More carried out in his own life. Education is universal, free to all, and continued through life. Books and reading constitute one of the chief pleasures of the whole community. Asceticism is rejected, and the Utopians believe that all pure and honest pleasures are meant by God to be enjoyed. Labour is prevented

5

from becoming monotonous by a constant change of occupation
from craftsmanship to agriculture, from life in the country to
life in the town.   The greatest reverence is paid by the young to
the old, the sick and suffering are diligently provided for, health
is regarded as the highest earthly good, and ensured by careful
measures of sanitation, and an attempt is made, in religious
matters, to combine public worship in rites agreeable to all, with
perfect liberty of conscience, and freedom to use in private any
form of worship.

It was only with great difficulty that such a man as the author
of the ' Utopia ' was at last persuaded by Henry VIII. to enter
his service.   More hated Court life, and loved simplicity, but the
Oxford Reformers had hope that the young and generous king
would aid in their plans of good government in Church and State.
There were no limits to Henry's admiration for More.   Like every
one else who knew him, he fell an easy victim to the charms of
that fascinating personality.   In spite of himself, More was drawn
to the Court to give advice to Henry on state business, to talk on
scholarship, astronomy, and theology, to keep the king and queen
and courtiers in continuous laughter by his gaiety and wit.   He
loathed it all the time, and longed for his Chelsea home. his books,
and his children.   "He tried," says Erasmus, "as hard to keep
out of court as most men do to get into it."   It is notable that in
order to escape from the company of kings and queens he had at
last to suppress his wit and become like other folk.   "When he
perceived," says his biographer, "that he could not once in a
month get leave to go home to his wife and children, he, much
misliking this restraint of liberty, began thereupon somewhat to
dissemble his nature, and so by little and little from his former mirth
to disuse himself, that he was of them from thenceforth no more so
ordinarily sent for."   The king visited him at his house at Chelsea,
nevertheless, heaped honours and offices upon him, making him
Treasurer of the Exchequer and Chancellor of the Duchy of
Lancaster, and not hesitating to astonish More's household by
walking for an hour in the garden with his arm round his subject's neck.   William Roper congratulated his father-in-law upon
his great good fortune.   But More was under no delusions, and

had already gauged the character of the king. "Son Roper," he said gravely, "I have no cause to be proud hereof. For if my head would win his Highness a castle in France, it should not fail to go off."

In 1523, the King and Wolsey contrived to have More made Speaker of the House of Commons. It was a critical time, and there were heavy subsidies to be demanded from Parliament. Once again, however, he was found in opposition to the Tudor monarchy, and, so far from aiding Wolsey, led the House of Commons to victory. In vain Wolsey broke out wrathfully, "Would to God, Master More, you had been at Rome when I made you speaker!" "Your grace not offended," answered Sir Thomas coolly, "so would I too, my lord." He was an opponent whom no taunts nor insults could sting into retaliation. Differing at the Council table on one occasion from Wolsey on some question of foreign policy, the Cardinal called More "the veriest fool in all the King's Council." "God be thanked," answered More, with quiet irony but no trace of anger, "that his Majesty hath only one fool in his Council."

There has come down to us a picture of the home life of More at this time, which is valuable both for what it tells us, and as a piece of literature from a master hand. It is found in one of the epistles of Erasmus. "More has built," he says, "near London, upon the Thames, a modest yet commodious mansion. There he lives surrounded by his family, including his wife, his son and his son's wife, his three daughters and their husbands, and eleven grand-children. There is not any man living so affectionate as he; and he loveth his old wife as if she were a girl of fifteen. In More's house, you would say that Plato's Academy was revived again, only whereas in the Academy the discussions turned upon geometry and the power of numbers, the house at Chelsea is a veritable school of Christian religion. In it is none, man or woman, but readeth or studieth the liberal arts, yet is their chief care of piety. There is never any seen idle. The head of the house governs it not by a lofty carriage and oft rebukes, but by gentleness and amiable manners. Every member is busy in his place, performing his duty with alacrity, nor is sober mirth wanting."

In 1529, on Wolsey's fall, More, much against his will, became
Lord Chancellor of England. It was not long, however, before he
found that there was the widest possible divergence of views
between Henry and himself upon the all-important subject of the
day, the divorce from Catherine of Arragon. In this matter the
King had hoped to have the support of More's great authority
upon his side, and was bitterly disappointed at the attitude of his
Chancellor, who firmly declined in any shape or form to
countenance the divorce. More had two reasons. He believed it
to be a gross injustice in itself, and furthermore he distrusted the
Protestant reformers, and would lend no aid to the destruction of
the Papal supremacy. With the King's consent he laid down his
office and went into retirement. He had entered Henry's service
a rich man: he left it without rewards of any kind, with an
income of £100 a year. The clergy, out of gratitude for the fierce
and violent books which More had written against the Protestants
of England and Germany, voted him a grant of £5,000. He
declined it, saying that he would rather see it all cast into the
Thames. He wanted neither riches nor honours, only rest and
peace.

The crisis of Sir Thomas More's life arrived when in the year
1533, Henry VIII., impatient of long years of delay in lawsuits
and Papal negotiations, cut the Gordian knot by marrying Anne
Boleyn, and in the teeth of all Europe proclaiming her as lawful
Queen of England. On January 25, Anne Boleyn gained the
object of her selfish ambition, and was secretly married to the
King. On the 23d of May, Thomas Cranmer, but lately created
Archbishop of Canterbury, with that ignoble subservience to his
sovereign which was the worst stain on his character, pronounced
sentence of divorce against Queen Catherine, and a week later
her rival was crowned at Westminster with magnificent pomp and
pageantry, such as England had never witnessed before. An
invitation to be present had been sent to the ex-Lord Chancellor,
together with a present of £20 to buy him a Court dress, he being
now reduced to poverty. More firmly refused, and thereby signed
his own death-warrant, as he knew. Henceforth he was a marked
and doomed man. The minister who now ruled both England

and Henry with a rod of iron was Thomas Cromwell, still the
unsolved riddle of Tudor history : a man of kindly temperament
in private life, but in government the Archfiend of Tyranny, a
faithful disciple of Machiavelli, cool, passionless, indomitable,
bent upon building up in England an absolute monarchy, and upon
making his sovereigns supreme in Church and State. It was with
an unerring instinct that the King and minister perceived that
the most formidable foe they had in England in their absolutist
designs was Sir Thomas More. Quietly and calmly, he had with-
drawn himself from their plans, but that was not enough. In
every country of Europe his name was famous. In England he
was respected and reverenced universally, and even his silent
opposition was dangerous to the government. Cromwell in singling
out the victims of his policy invariably pursued the same method :
he let the weak and the inconsiderable and the mean go free, and
struck at the greatest and the noblest, the leaders of men. So it
happened that one of the first sufferers under the English Reign
of Terror was Sir Thomas More.

I will not weary you by tracing out the various devices which
were used to betray the noblest of Englishmen to his death. One
or two examples must suffice. His enemies were foolish enough
in their malice to charge the purest judge the nation had possessed
for two centuries with receiving bribes and presents from suitors
in his court. An inquiry was held, and every accusation was
triumphantly refuted. It was proved beyond doubt that, after
the evil custom of the time, persons who had gained favourable
verdicts at his hand, had presented him with valuable gifts. It
was also proved that Sir Thomas More, unlike his fellow-judges,
had returned them every one. Next, an unsuccessful endeavour
was made to implicate him in the treasonable speeches of the
Romanist prophetess, Elizabeth Barton, the Nun of Kent.
Parliament passed an Act of Attainder against her, and the King
had determined that More should be included as one of her
accomplices; but the charge was so false and monstrous, that his
own ministers on their knees persuaded him to omit More's name,
assuring him that the House of Lords would never find him
guilty. Threats and persuasions alike were tried with the late

Chancellor, but all in vain. Almost alone in that immoral age, More allowed himself the luxury of a conscience, and he was steadfastly resolved never at the bidding of a tyrant king to declare that to be right which he knew to be wrong. He looked death in the face and calmly made his decision, smiling when the Duke of Norfolk, alarmed at his danger, gave him a friendly hint. " By the mass, Mr. More," the Duke had said, " it is perilous striving with Princes, and therefore I would wish you to incline to the King's pleasure. The anger of a monarch means death." " Is that all, my lord ? " More replied ; " then there is no more difference between your grace and me but that I shall die to-day and you to-morrow." The resources of tyranny, however, were not exhausted, and Cromwell had more dangerous weapons to use than these. In 1534 there was passed an Act of Succession, excluding the Princess Mary from the throne, declaring Anne Boleyn Queen, and settling the crown upon her children. In itself that statute was powerless to hurt More, who acknowledged fully, as a loyal Englishman, the right of Parliament to determine the succession. But by another provision of the same statute, manifestly aimed at More and those who believed as he did, the King was empowered to administer to any subject in the realm an oath which declared his marriage with Catherine of Arragon to have been against Scripture and invalid from the beginning. It was well known that More could take no such oath. But on April 13, 1534, while at Chelsea, he was summoned by Cranmer to appear at Lambeth and receive it. There was a sharp, short struggle. More was no ambitious candidate for the honours of martyrdom, and there were reasons enough, in his sweet home life at Chelsea, amidst his children and grandchildren, his books and his friends, with Margaret Roper, the true and perfect ideal of English womanhood, ever at his side, and the great Erasmus and half the learned men of Europe for his intellectual companions—reasons enough, surely, to make him hesitate. Why should he not do what bishops and nobles had not disdained to do, and earn peace and rest by going through a mere form of words ? The King, he knew, would prevail in the end. Why should he maintain, singlehanded, a hopeless opposition ? No such pleadings had any weight with More. "Never," said Erasmus, "did Nature mould a temper more gentle, endearing, and happy than the temper of Thomas More." It was true, but it was also true that never since the days when King Alfred the Truth-teller reigned in England, had there been an Englishman endowed with a stronger will and more indomitable spirit. Beneath all his laughter and gaiety, there lurked an iron determination and the courage of a martyr. The struggle within him was soon over, and in the end life and love and happiness seemed less precious than honour and duty and a manful struggle against unlawful tyranny. Let me read to you William Roper's touching account of this mental conflict. He was with him at Chelsea when the summons came. "Whereas," he says, "Sir Thomas More used evermore at his departure from his house and children (whom he loved tenderly) to have them bring him to his boat, and there to kiss them all and bid them farewell, at this time would he suffer none of them forth of the gate to follow him, but pulled the wicket after him, and shut them all from him, and with a heavy heart (as by his countenance it appeared) with me and our four servants then took his boat towards Lambeth. Wherein sitting still sadly awhile, at the last he rounded me in the ear and said, 'Son Roper, I thank our Lord, the field is won.'"

At Lambeth More remained resolute. He would obey the laws, he said, and acknowledge the succession, but he could not perjure himself by taking the oath, which contained matter that he did not believe. In vain Cranmer plied him with arguments and subtle distinctions. He finally declined to obey, and was committed to the Tower.

There he remained for a whole year in harsh and severe imprisonment, surrounded by spies, who endeavoured to entrap him in treasonable words, troubled somewhat by the complaints and commonplace pleadings of his worldly wife, Dame Alice. She "marvelled," she said, "that he who had always hitherto been taken for so wise a man, should now so play the fool as to lie in a close, filthy prison, when he might be abroad at his liberty, in favour with King and Council, if he would but do as all the Bishops and best learned of the realm had done." There was one,

however, whose pure nature and lofty soul could understand that a
noble man might value his life less than a conscience free from
blame; and amid his long, weary imprisonment, More was constantly cheered and encouraged in his resolution by her who would
gladly have laid down her life for his, his daughter Margaret.

At last, in May, 1535, he was placed on his trial at Westminster,
charged with new treasons in having denied the King's title as
Supreme Head of the Church. New weapons for the removal of
opponents had now been placed in the hands of the King and
Cromwell. Not only had Henry been declared Head of the
Church, but Parliament had passed an outrageous law inflicting
all the penalties of high treason upon any person who should deny
any of his titles, and the lawyers had twisted this to mean that
positive guilt need not be proved. If a man refused to answer
official questions concerning his belief about the Supremacy, that
was sufficient. Even Mr. Froude, who is not particular about
strong measures, apologizes for this infamous statute, and admits
that it bordered upon oppression. I dwell upon it because it is
important to notice exactly what it was that More declined to do
and for what cause he was put to death. It is usually said that he
was executed because he denied the King's Supremacy. It would
be more accurate to say that he died because he refused to answer
questions as to his private belief on the matter. He scrupulously
avoided writing or speaking against the Act of Supremacy. He
was put to death for keeping silence.

The details of his trial need not concern us. It was, perhaps,
the worst of the judicial murders of Henry's reign. The result
was a foregone conclusion. The prosecutors for the Crown were
themselves the witnesses. The only shred of evidence against
More was given by Solicitor-General Rich, a man of bad life
and character. The jury, notwithstanding, after fifteen minutes
deliberation, found More guilty, and he was condemned to death,
Lord Chancellor Audley intimating that the King, out of his
gracious favour to him, had been pleased to change the usual
punishment for treason to beheading. "God forbid," said More,
with the wit that never failed him, " that the King should shew
any more such mercy unto any of my friends; and God preserve

my posterity from all such pardons." No words of bitterness or
condemnation against the men who had just consigned him to
death escaped him, and with a smile he took farewell of his
judges. "My lords," he said, "I verily trust that though your
lordships have been on earth judges to my condemnation, we
may yet hereafter in heaven meet merrily together to our ever-
lasting salvation. God preserve you all, especially my sovereign
lord the King, and send him faithful councillors."

A harder trial awaited him. As he landed at the Tower Wharf,
his daughter Margaret, who had watched for him there to take her
last farewell, without care for herself thrust aside the weapons of
the guards and fell at her father's feet asking his blessing. "The
beholding whereof," says Roper, "was to many of them that were
present thereat so lamentable, that it made them for very sorrow
to mourn and to weep." For More, when his daughter at last
was constrained to leave him, the bitterness of death was past.

A week later they led him forth to die. The imprisonment in
the Tower had done its work. His hair was now sprinkled with
grey, his body emaciated, and it was with difficulty that he walked
to the place of execution. No physical weakness, however, could
bend his lofty spirit nor mar the splendid courage with which he
met his death. Historians have wondered at the extraordinary
composure which he displayed, and some have censured his levity.
The truth is that to no Englishman who ever lived did the change
from life to death seem so slight as to Sir Thomas More. "His
death," it has been well said by Addison, "was of a piece with his
life. There was nothing in it new, forced, or affected. The
innocent mirth which had been so conspicuous in his life did not
forsake him to the last."

As he placed his foot upon the ladder, the scaffold, which had
been badly put together, shook and seemed likely to fall. More
turned with a smile to his friend, Sir William Kingston, the
Lieutenant of the Tower. "Master Lieutenant," he said, perhaps
with a kindly intention to cheer his friend, "I pray you see me
safe up, and for my coming down let me shift for myself." The
executioner begged his forgiveness. "Thou art about to do me,"
said More, "a greater service this day than ever any mortal man

can give me." Then, having declared to the people that he died in the faith of the Holy Catholic Church and a faithful servant to God and the king, he repeated the Miserere Psalm, and binding a cloth over his eyes, knelt at the block. The headsman was about to strike, when More signed to him to delay while he removed his beard. "Pity," he murmured, not in levity but saddest irony, "pity that should be cut which never committed treason."

"With which strange words," writes Mr. Froude, compelled for once to be generous, "the strangest perhaps ever uttered at such a time, the lips most famous through Europe for eloquence and wisdom closed forever. . . . . Something of his calmness may have been due to his natural temperament, something to an unaffected weariness of a world which in his eyes was plunging into the ruin of the latter days. But those fair hues of sunny cheerfulness caught their colour from the simplicity of his faith; and never was there a Christian's victory over death more grandly evidenced than in that last scene lighted with its lambent humour."

Beautiful, surely, this life. Beautiful, this joyous death. But it is not for those things only that I have ventured to commend Sir Thomas More's history to your notice. It is this noble book of his, this 'Utopia,' deserving, if ever volume did, John Milton's description of a good book, "the precious life-blood of a master-spirit, embalmed and treasured up to a life beyond life," which constitutes in this age More's chief claim to our regard. We live in a time when humanity is throbbing with new ideals and new aspirations, when especially one fresh hope animates the world, that in the near future the hard lot of the suffering, patient millions who bear the burden of the earth's toil shall be ameliorated. We are not worthy to live in our generation—I dare to say it—if we have no share in this hope. We are no true students of the Extension movement if in some degree we do not share the enthusiasm and the spirit of Sir Thomas More. This movement of ours—let us openly proclaim what many of you have discovered already—is in its essence a movement for Social Reform. That does not mean that it need create apprehension in the mind of any one. We are no Revolutionists. We have no party politics to propagate. There are no valued institutions of our country which we wish to assail. We give allegiance to no Socialism except the Socialism of Jesus Christ. We do not believe that Christianity is an exploded myth. Our methods in their degree are the methods of the Oxford Reformers—of Colet and Erasmus and More. What we care about mainly is that the best gifts of God shall be scattered broadcast amongst the people; that culture and knowledge and exalted ideals shall spread from the few to the many; that " no man shall die ignorant to whom God has given the capacity for knowledge; " that the great cities shall not long continue the scandal and the shame alike of our Religion and our Humanity.

" *Oh ! why, and for what, are we waiting, while our brothers droop*
   and die,

   And on every wind of the heavens a wasted life goes by !

   How long shall they reproach us, where crowd on crowd they
      dwell,

   Poor ghosts of the wicked city, the gold-crushed, hungry hell !

   *   *   *   *   *   *

   They are gone ! There is none can undo it, nor save our souls
      from the curse ;

   But many a million cometh, and shall they be better, or worse ! "

(*a*)—CONTEMPORARIES OF THE OXFORD REFORMERS (1466—1536).

Richard III.	1452—1485.	Savonarola	1452—1498.
Henry VIII.	1491—1547.	Michael Angelo	1475—1564.
Francis I.	1494—1547.	Raphael	1483—1520.
Charles V.	1500—1558.	Machiavelli	1469—1527.
Alexander VI.	1431—1503.	Pico della Mirandola	1463—1494.
Leo X.	1475—1523.	Rabelais	1495—1553.
Columbus	1435—1506.	Luther	1483—1546.
Copernicus	1473—1543.	Zwingle	1484—1531.
Gutenberg	1410—1468.	Tyndale	1484—1536.
Caxton	1422—1491.	Loyola	1491—1556.

(*b*)—HISTORICAL EVENTS DURING COLET'S LIFETIME.

Battle of Tewkesbury	1471.
Death of Charles the Bold	1477.
Battle of Bosworth	1485.
Spaniards enter Grenada	1492.
Columbus discovers S. Salvador	1492.
Charles VIII. invades Italy	1494.
Cabot discovers coast of North America	1497.
Execution of Savonarola	1498.
Leo X. becomes Pope	1513.
Luther writes his Wittenberg theses	1517.

(*c*)—THE REVIVAL OF LEARNING IN ENGLAND.

" It is never among the people who give birth to new ideas that those ideas attain to their healthiest development. The new thought takes possession of them too exclusively, and quickens one side of their nature into too one-sided a life. So it had been in the early Middle Ages with the monasticism of the East. So it was when the Middle Ages drew to a close with the Humanism of Italy. What Benedict of Nursia was to Simeon Stylites, Colet and More were to Pulci and Machiavelli. The Italians had before them the lees of Mediæval Christianity in their foulest corruption. Their reverence for humanity grew to be mere pampering of the intellect or of the senses. In England, as the evil was less intense, the reaction was less intense also. The old Church life lived on in the words of Colet, interpenetrated with a new spirit of inquiry and a new longing for a reign of justice rather than for self-mortification."

S. R. GARDINER.

(*d*)—COLET'S PROGRAMME FOR REFORM IN THE CHURCH.

" Let those lawes be rehersed that do warne you fathers that ye put not over soone your hands on every man, or admitte into holy orders. . . . Let the lawes be rehersed that commande that benefices of the church be gyven to those that are worthy; and that promotions be made in the churche by the ryghte balance of vertue, not by carnall affection: whereby this happeneth nowe-a days that boyes for olde men, fooles for wise men, euyll for good, do reigne and rule. . . . Let the lawes be rehersed that warreth against the spot of Symonie . . . that commande personall residence of curates in theyre churches . . . that command that the goodes of the church be spent, nat in costly byldyng, nat in sumptuous apparrell and pompis, nat in feastyng and bankettynge, nat in excesse and wantonnes, nat in enrichinge of kynsfolke, nat in kepynge of dogges, but in things profitable and necessary to the churche . . . Let the lawes be rehersed of the residence of bysshops in theyr diocesis; that commande that they loke diligently, and take hede to the helthe of soules; that they shew themselves in their churches at the leest on greatte holye-dayes; that they here the causes and matters of poure men; that they sustein fatherles children and widowes; that they exercise them selfe in workes of virtue."

Convocation Sermon of 1512.

(*e*)—COLET AND S. PAUL'S SCHOOL.

" I pray God all may be to his honour, and to the erudicyon and profyt of chyldren my countrie-men, Londoners specyally, whome dygestynge this lytel werke I had alwaye before mine eyen, consyderinge more what was for them than to shewe any grete connynge, wyllyng to speke the thynges often before spoken in suche maner as gladly yonge begynners and tender wittes myght take and conceyue. Wherefore I pray you, al lytel babys, al lytel children, lerne gladly this lytel treatise, and commende it dylygently vnto your memoryes. Trustynge of this begynninge that ye shal procede and growe to parfyt lyterature, and come at last to be gret clarkes. And lyfte vp your lytel whyte hands for me, which prayeth for you to God. To whom be al honour and imperyal maieste and glory. Amen."

'A lytell proheme to the boke ' (Colet's Accidence.)

(*f*)—The Chief Works of Erasmus.

Enchiridion Militis Christiani .	1503.	Adagia	1500—1520.
Praise of Folly	1510.	Institutio Principis Christiani . .	1516.
Novum Instrumentum	1516.	Paraphrase of the New Testament 1519.	
Treatise on Free-Will	1524.	Familiar Colloquies . . .	1519—1530.

"Desiderius Erasmus. Auctor damnatus. Opera omnia Erasmi caute legenda, tam multa enim insunt correctione digna ut vix omnia expurgari possint." 'Index Expurgatorius.'

(*g*)—Erasmus on War.

"Oh! that God would be merciful and still this storm which is raging in the Christian world. We are worse than the dumb animals, for among them it is only the wild beasts that wage war, and that with the weapons with which nature has furnished them; not as we do with machines invented by the art of the devil. Can we who glory in the name of Christ, whose precepts and example taught us only gentleness, think anything in this world of such value that it should provoke us to war ?—a thing so ruinous, so hateful, that even when it is most just, no truly good man can approve of it, carried on as it is by homicides, gamblers, scoundrels of every kind, by the lowest class of hirelings, who care more for a little gain than for their lives." Ep. to Anthony à Bergis, 1514.

(*h*)—His Attack on Regal Tyranny.

"Princes should be chosen, not taken at random, as they are now: the result being that the people build cities, princes destroy them; the industry of citizens enriches the state, which the princes' rapacity plunders; popular magistrates enact good laws for kings to break; the people love peace, and their rulers stir up war." 'Adagia.'

(*i*)—His Theory of the Papacy.

"The Roman Pontiff is the chief herald of the Gospel, as other bishops are his heralds. All bishops are vicegerents of Christ, but among them the Roman Pontiff is pre-eminent. But they are his worst enemies who ascribe to him, in order to flatter him, an authority which he himself does not claim, and which it is not for the advantage of the Christian flock that he should possess." Ep. to Archbishop of Maintz, 1519.

(*j*)—His Hatred of Dogma.

"Let us have done with theological refinements. A man is not lost because he cannot tell whether the Spirit has one principle or two. Has he the fruits of the Spirit? That is the question. Is he patient, kind, good, gentle, modest, temperate, chaste? Inquire if you will, but do not define. True religion is peace, and we cannot have peace unless we leave the conscience unshackled on obscure points on which certainty is impossible." Ep. to Arch. of Palermo, 1523.

(*k*)—His Relations to Luther and the Reformation.

"I neither approve Luther nor condemn him. If he is innocent, he ought not to be oppressed by the factions of the wicked; if he is in error, he should be answered, not destroyed. The theologians do not try to answer him. They do but raise an insane and senseless clamour, and shriek and curse." Ep. to the Prince Elector Albert, 1519.

"As to your advice that I should join Luther, there will be no difficulty about that, should I find him on the side of the Catholic Church. But if matters shall come to extremities, and a revolution take place, by which the Church shall be made to totter on her throne, I will in the meantime anchor myself to that solid rock until it shall become clear on the restoration of peace where the Church is, and wherever there is evangelical peace there will Erasmus be found." Letter of 1521.

"I am ready to be a martyr for Christ, if He give me strength to do so; but I have no wish to be a martyr for Luther."
Ep. to Ulric von Hutten, 1523.

"My aim is the advancement of literature, and a pure simple theology. I ask not whether Luther approve or not; Luther and this generation shall pass away, but Christ abideth for ever." Answer to Hutten, 1523.

(*l*)—Erasmus' Estimate of More.

"If you want a perfect pattern of real friendship, you must look for it in More. He has so much affability, and suavity of manner, that there is no one, however morose may be his disposition, whom he does not make cheerful. . . There is nothing in the world, however serious it may be, from which he does not extract pleasantry. If he has intercourse with wise and learned men, he is delighted with their genius; if with unlearned and foolish men, he enjoys their folly. . . No one is less swayed by the opinions of the world, and no one is more remarkable for common sense. . . From early life he has loved the pursuit of letters. . . He is altogether without pride, and in the midst of weighty affairs of State he remembers his old friends, and returns to his beloved literature. . . John Colet, a man of shrewdness and accurate judgment, says of him in conversation, that there is but one genius in England, and that his name is Thomas More. He is a man of real piety, very remote from all superstition. He converses in such a manner with his friends respecting the world to come, that you see at once that he has a hope full of immortality."
Letter to Ulric von Hutten, 1519.

(*m*)—More's Attack on the Social Conditions of his Time.

"Is not this an vniust and an unkynde publyke weale, whyche gyueth great fees and rewardes to gentlemen, as they call them, and to gold smythes, and to suche other, whiche be either ydle persones, or els onlye flatterers, and deuysers of vain pleasures : And of the contrary parte maketh no gentle prouision for poore ploumen, coliars, laborers, carters, yronsmythes, and carpenters : without whome no commen wealthe can contineue ? But after it hath abused the labours of theire lusty and glowing age, at the laste when they be oppressed with olde age and sickenes : being nedye, poore, and indigent of all things, then forgetting theire so manye and so greate benefits recompenseth and acquyteth them moste vnkyndly with miserable death. And yet besides this the riche men not only by private fraud, but also by commen lawes, do euery day pluck and snatche awaye from the poor some part of their daily liuing. . . Therefore when I consider and way in my mind all these commen wealthes, which now a dayes any where do flourish, so God helpe me, I can perceaue nothing but a certein conspiracy of riche men procuringe their owne commodities vnder the name and title of the common wealth."   'Utopia.'

(*n*)—SATIRE OF THE ' UTOPIA.'

" In Utopia all the priests are of exceeding holiness, and therefore their number is but few."

" Furthermore, they utterly exclude and banish all attorneys, proctors, and sergeants at the law, which craftily handle matters and subtilly dispute of the laws. For they think it most meet that every man should plead his own matter, and tell the same tale before the judge that he would tell to his man of law."

" Princely virtue, which like as it is of much higher majesty than poor folks' virtue, so also it is of much more liberty, as to the which nothing is unlawful that it lusteth after."

" They gather pearls by the seaside, and diamonds and carbuncles upon certain rocks, and with these they deck their young infants, which when they be grown in years do lay them by, perceiving that none but children do wear such toys and trifles."

" They count hunting the lowest, the vilest, and most abject part of butchery, and the other parts of it more profitable, and most honest, as bringing much more commodity, in that they kill beasts only for necessity."

" They hire soldiers from all places, but chiefly from the Zapoletæ (Swiss), a hardy race, born only for war, ready to serve any prince that will hire them, in great numbers. They know none of the arts of life except how to take it away. They serve their employers actively and faithfully . . . but they will change sides for the advance of a halfpenny. As the Utopians look out for good men for their own use at home, they employ the greatest scoundrels abroad : and they think they do a great service to mankind by thus ridding the world of the entire scum of such a foul and nefarious population."

                                                   'Utopia,' Book II.

(*o*)—Doctrines of Religious Toleration in the 'Utopia.'

" This is one of the ancientest laws among them : that no man shall be blamed for reasoning in the maintenance of his own religion. For King Utopus, even at the first beginning, hearing that the inhabitants of the land were, before his coming thither, at continual dissension and strife among themselves for their religions : first of all, made a decree that it should be lawful for every man to favour and follow what religion he would, and that he might do the best he could to bring others to his opinion, so that he did it peaceably, gently, quietly, and soberly, without hasty and contentious rebuking and inveighing against other. If he could not by fair and gentle speech induce them into his opinion, yet he should use no kind of violence, and refrain from displeasant and seditious words. . . . Therefore he gave to every man free liberty and choice to believe what he would, saving that he earnestly charged them that no man should conceive so vile and base an opinion of the dignity of man's nature, as to think that the souls do die and perish with the bodies. . . . He that is thus minded is deprived of all honours, excluded from all common administrations in the weal public. . . . Howbeit they put him to no punishment, because they be persuaded, that it is no man's power to believe what he list."

Books.

(a)—Text Books.

    i. F. Seebohm's Oxford Reformers. (Longmans.)
    ii.   "   Era of the Protestant Revolution. (Longmans.)
    iii. Green's Short History of the English People. (Macmillan.)
    iv. More's Utopia, edited by J. R. Lumby. (Cambridge Press.)
    v. Life of Erasmus, by Rev. A. R. Pennington. (Seeley.)

(b)—Biographies.

    i. Life of John Colet, by Rev. J. H. Lupton. (Bell & Sons.)
    Lives of Vitrarius and Colet, by Erasmus, edited by Lupton.
    Life, by Dr. S. Knight. (Oxford, 1823.)
    ii. Life and Character of Erasmus, by R. B. Drummond. 2 vols. 1873.
    Jortin's Life of Erasmus. 2 vols. 1758.
    iii. Roper's Life of More (included in Lumby's edition of the Utopia).
    Cresacre More's Life of More. 1627.
    Stapleton's Tres Thomæ. 1588.
    Life by Sir James Macintosh. 1844.
    Life by Father Bridgett, S. J., 1891.

(c)—Essays.

    i. Articles on More and Erasmus in Encyclopædia Britannica, by M. Pattison.
    ii. Essay on Erasmus, by Milman.
    iii. Times of Erasmus and Luther, by J. A. Froude. (Short Studies. Vol. 1).
    iv. Erasmus. Oxford Prize Essay, by A. L. Smith.

(d)—Works.

    i. Colet's lectures have been edited by Mr. Lupton.
    The Convocation sermon is printed in Blunt's History of the Reformation, Vol. 1.

ii. Works of Erasmus, edited by Le Clerc. 10 vols. 1703.

The 'Praise of Folly,' and the 'Colloquies' can be read in English translations.

The most important of the Epistles of Erasmus are translated in Drummond's Life.

iii. More's Collected Works. 1689.

Utopia. Best reprint is Arber's. 1869.

(*e*)—HISTORIES AND BOOKS OF REFERENCE.

i. Brewer's Reign of Henry VIII. 2 vols. 1884.

ii. Froude's History of England. Vols. I., II.

iii. Dixon's History of the Reformation.

iv. Hibbert Lectures for 1883, by Dr. C. Beard.

v. Symonds' Renaissance in Italy.

vi. Lingard's History of England.

vii. Nisard. Etudes sur la Renaissance.

viii. Niccolò Machiavelli and his Times. Pasquale Villari.

ix. Villari's Life of Savonarola.

x. Köstlin's Life of Luther.

Lightning Source UK Ltd.
Milton Keynes UK
UKHW020025181218
334174UK00013B/2019/P

9 780331 812640